ABRAHAM LINCOLN
AND
WALT WHITMAN

Photo by Brady

ABRAHAM LINCOLN AS WALT WHITMAN LIKED TO REMEMBER HIM

Abraham Lincoln

and

Walt Whitman

By

WILLIAM E. BARTON

*Author of The Life of Abraham Lincoln,
The Women Lincoln Loved, Etc.*

Illustrated

KENNIKAT PRESS
Port Washington, New York

ABRAHAM LINCOLN AND WALT WHITMAN

To
CLARK PRESCOTT BISSETT
WHOSE WORK I ADMIRE AND
WHOSE FRIENDSHIP I VALUE

FOREWORD

THIS book had its inception in the discovery, by Mr. William Adams Slade, Chief Bibliographer of the Library of Congress, of what seemed to both of us to be an utterly unknown lecture on Abraham Lincoln by Walt Whitman. I asked Mr. Slade if he did not intend to publish this himself, and he replied that he was too busy assisting other people in their publications and that I was welcome to what he had found. The generosity of librarians is one of my most sincere acknowledgments.

It proved, however, that our discovery was not quite all that we had thought. It was an earlier form of what, considerably enlarged and somewhat revised, appeared in *Specimen Days and Collect* as Whitman's lecture on the death of Lincoln. But it was evidently set up from Walt's own manuscript, furnished for that purpose to the *New York Tribune*.

I set forth to discover how it happened that Walt prepared this lecture, and through what stages of development its evolution could be traced. How many times did he deliver it? How much did he change it? Were any interesting incidents on record concerning any of the occasions when he read it? I began to gather some information in answer to questions such as these.

But I also asked: Did Walt originally prepare this as a lecture? Crippled as he was, had he at first a purpose to set forth in a career upon the platform? I found the substance of the lecture still earlier, in the *New York Sun,* there described as a chapter in a forthcoming book.

Earlier still, I found the germ of it in his *Memoranda of the Civil War,* alleged to have been written on the spot, but not necessarily much earlier in its form than the date of its publication, 1876.

By this time I was ready for more thorough search in the Library of Congress, and that in the Manuscripts Division. Large is my debt to Dr. Herbert Putnam, Chief Librarian, and to Dr. Charles Moore, then Chief of the Manuscripts Division, and his first Assistant, the present acting chief, Mr. John C. Fitzpatrick, for courtesies extending over many years.

The Whitman manuscripts are a Slough of Despond. No one had ever sorted them, and he will be a courageous man who undertakes this task. But I undertook to find everything about Lincoln that was contained in this mass of stromata, and so far as possible to assemble the scraps and shreds in order. The Library has carefully mounted these odds and ends of Lincoln material as I assembled it, and made an attractive

book of it. These fragments show the evolution of
the Lincoln lecture, and like the stones of
Jericho, they are there unto this day. I undertook
also to obtain an adequate background in Walt's
own experience as far as these manuscripts disclose it, and at least I found some things which,
as far as I am aware, have not been discovered by
others.

I asked such questions as these: What, if anything, did Walt write about Lincoln while Lincoln
was living? What was his honest judgment at the
time when he and Lincoln were both residents of
Washington? What did he say in print, if anything? What did he say in his home letters, and in
his diaries, before he edited them for publication?

This inevitably led me to inquire how truthful
Walt Whitman was, and I am sorry to have
discovered as much negative evidence as I did. I
do not think Walt was a liar; he merely lied.

I had to ask also: How much did Whitman
actually see of Lincoln? And: How much did
Lincoln know about Whitman?

I could not depend on Walt's biographers. My
collection of Whitmaniana, still microscopic compared with my Lincoln collection, grew to a quite
respectable size. I was welcomed to the stacks of
the Boston Public Library, within reach of my
summer home. And I found that Walt's own
quality of exaggeration and general inaccuracy
had been shared by most of the men who wrote

about him. The chief exceptions among his biographers, as I think, are Prof. Bliss Perry and Prof. Emory Holloway. Even they accept Walt's own statements in matters where I found him to be romancing. But Perry and Holloway have honestly sought to tell the truth; the most of those who write about him attempt simply to glorify Walt Whitman.

I was very sorry to have to give up the story that Lincoln looked out of the White House window and saw Walt, and said, "He looks like a man." Walt did look like a man, and Lincoln was a competent judge of manhood, and the sentence sounded like Lincoln. Mr. Oscar Lion, owner of the manuscript on which this story depends, permitted me access to his manuscripts, with the result that this book shows.

I succeeded in making what appears to be a definitive study of the Lincoln lecture. I think I have discovered how it began, and through what stages it developed, and I am able to show its evolution in this volume. To save the somewhat wearisome process of repetition in the text, I have carried part of this material over into the Appendix, where it can be studied for purposes of comparison without unduly loading the narrative. I do not know where anything of importance is now to be learned on that aspect of my search.

But this inevitably led me into a study of Whitman's poems on Lincoln, and so into an effort to find everything that Whitman ever wrote or said about him, so far as this could be discovered. And this led into a study of Walt's whole life.

I have already written the life-story of Lincoln, and I have restrained myself from writing a biography of Walt Whitman. But I have undertaken to relate so much of Whitman's life-story as is connected with his writings on Lincoln, and this has involved some consideration of the aim and spirit of his writings as a whole, and particularly his interpretation of the spirit of America, as he found it incarnate in Abraham Lincoln.

Inevitably I had to make comparisons of the two men. They were contemporaries and they had many qualities in common, and some in sharp contrast. When I had finished the chapter in which I set their characters alongside for a study of the elements in each that remind us of the other, I had some feeling that perhaps that chapter might stand as a contribution toward an understanding of the two men.

If I shall be accused of any lack of charity with regard to the moral character of Whitman, it is not likely that the criticism will come from any who know the facts. I could have said more if it had been necessary. It was not necessary, for I have not set out to pass judgment on Whitman except as such judgment becomes essential to a right understanding of his relations to the life of Lincoln. All men have faults, and the faults of men of large

nature are not usually small faults. With all his
faults, I like Walt Whitman.

In the matter of Walt Whitman's hospital service, and the literature resulting from or related to
it, I had a special interest and something of a background of knowledge which appear to me to have
been of some value. I do not discover that any of
Walt Whitman's friends at the time of the Civil
War or later accompanied him frequently on his
hospital visits, or knew about them except as they
learned from him. I also lacked the privilege of
going with him in person.

But it fell to me a few years ago to write the
Life of Clara Barton, founder of the American
Red Cross, and this involved the critical examination of the contents of two huge vaults crammed
with her papers. Virtually everything concerning
the management of Civil War hospitals was stored
away among those records, pamphlets, newspaper
clippings and letters. If I did not learn a great
deal about the care of the sick and wounded during
the Civil War, it was certainly my own fault. This
much at least I learned, that very much had been
published about the Washington hospitals and
Walt's possible connection with them was either
wholly imaginary or very greatly exaggerated.

I mention the matter here, because, if I am to
part company with other men who have written on
the subject, and who were closer to Walt Whitman
than it was ever my privilege to have been, I have

at least learned some things about the agencies that ministered to the wounded and the sick during the days when Walt was in Washington and making his contribution to this form of service. The romance of nursing sick soldiers attracted multitudes of men who preferred that work to fighting, and of sentimental women who thought the work romantic. Dorothea Dix drove most of them away, as Florence Nightingale also did in her day, and Clara Barton had little use for the vast majority of them. Not many stayed long. Walt Whitman remained. And I am confident that when all deductions have been made for his indolent and desultory way of doing whatever he did, and for his exaggeration and that of his biographers, he did much good work. Otherwise he would not have remained, and would not have been permitted to remain.

The publishers of the *North American Review* are generously permitting me to include in this volume Walt Whitman's article on Lincoln which first appeared in that magazine and afterward in their volume of *Reminiscences of Abraham Lincoln*. Quotations from Whitman's published writings, where not otherwise credited, are from his *Complete Prose Works,* and from *Leaves of Grass, Inclusive Edition,* edited by Prof. Emory Holloway. By his kind permission and that of the publishers, Doubleday Page and Company, these quotations are made. A number of his poems

FOREWORD

which, as far as I know, have never been printed
are here as I copied them from the Whitman manuscripts in the Library of Congress.

For portraits in this volume, I am under obligation to my friend, Frederick Hill Meserve, to
whom my debt already was large, and I hope to
increase it in the favors I intend to ask from him
in the making of other books. His collection of
American photographs is vast, and he knows what
he has, and is generous.

The epic of America is written, so far as it is
written, in divers portions and in sundry manners.
Abraham Lincoln wrote a chapter, and Walt
Whitman wrote some stanzas which are essential
to it. I am glad to have caught some portions of
their contribution toward the record of America
in one of its big blundering epochs, through which,
though of another generation, my own life thus far
has been lived.

WILLIAM E. BARTON

The Lincoln Room,
Pine Knoll on Sunset Lake,
Foxboro, Massachusetts.

CONTENTS

LIST OF ILLUSTRATIONS

ABRAHAM LINCOLN
AND
WALT WHITMAN

ABRAHAM LINCOLN AND
WALT WHITMAN

I

WALT WHITMAN ARRIVES IN WASHINGTON

As a rule, Walt Whitman enjoyed riding on ferry-boats, but to all rules there are exceptions. He had to employ two ferries to reach the train for Washington. The first conveyed him from Brooklyn to New York, and the second across the Hudson River to the New Jersey shore. It was a bleak cold day, and he was preoccupied and anxious. It seemed a long way, and he was nervous lest he should miss his train.

On the preceding day, Monday, the Whitman family learned of a terrible battle that had been fought at Fredericksburg on Saturday, December 13, 1862, and Walt's brother, Captain George Washington Whitman of the Fifty-first New York Volunteers, was reported among the injured. Walt did not know how badly George was wounded, but he made haste to start for Washing-

19

ton, where the wounded were said to be arriving as they were carried back from the front.

He arrived in Jersey City in time for his train, and sat through what was left of the short dark forenoon with very few inspiring thoughts. He did not know where he was to find George, nor whether George would be living or dead.

At Philadelphia the train stopped for refreshments, and Walt got out for his midday meal. When he reached the train, his pocketbook was missing. He believed that he had been robbed. He had his ticket, fortunately, but not a cent in money. It was a gloomy day.

He had ample time to think as the train crept along toward Washington. This journey was for him a long one. He had not been a great traveler. Born on Long Island on May 31, 1819, he had lived in Brooklyn practically his entire life since he was four. He had made a visit to New Orleans, but he did not remain long. He was now forty-three. He had been a carpenter, a schoolteacher, an editor, and had not done very well at any of these trades or professions. He was a printer, and had set up with his own hands the type for a book which he described as poetry, but which most people who attempted to read it refused to call by that name. The volume was a tall thin quarto, quite unusual in shape, and was entitled *Leaves of Grass*. It was published in 1855, and Walt had determined that his work thenceforth should be "the making of poems." Several of the reviews were highly complimentary, for Walt wrote them himself. A very few other people spoke well of the book.

In an incautious moment, Ralph Waldo Emerson wrote to him a letter of commendation. Walt selected the important sentence out of that communication, and caused it to be stamped in large letters on the backbone of the second edition—"I Greet You at the Beginning of a Great Career—R. W. EMERSON." People were surprised to see that legend on the cover of Walt's book, and no one so much so as Emerson. He could not deny that he had said it, but he never fully trusted Walt afterward.

This second edition, published in June, 1856, had been a fat duodecimo of three hundred and eighty-four pages. Like the first edition it bore no publisher's name. Fowler and Wells manufactured it, but refused to sell it. A third edition came out in 1860, bearing the imprint of Thayer and Eldridge of Boston, and it helped to send that firm into bankruptcy. None of the editions had sold well, and, while Walt was working on a new book called *Drum-Taps,* he had no publisher in sight.[1]

He had continued to live with his mother in Brooklyn, and had employment more or less steadily on newspapers. This occupation brought him free theater tickets, and a wide sidewalk acquaintance in Brooklyn and New York. He was

a "caresser of life," and he caressed life the better
when he had a full beer glass at Pfaff's, and a
company of cheerful friends.

Some of these friends were men, but not all. He
lived "jolly bodily," and, although the background of his life was Quaker, he had no religious
scruples that governed his habits in these matters.
He was unmarried. He did not desire to assume
responsibilities.

Walt had never been able to convince his own
family that what he wrote was poetry. His father,
the elder Walter Whitman, died on July 11, 1855,
the very month in which *Leaves of Grass* came
from the press in its first edition. What he would
have thought of it, we do not know. "I saw the
book," said his brother George, the same brother
Walt was on his way to discover, living or dead,
that day in December, 1862, "I saw the book,
didn't read it at all, didn't think it worth reading.
Mother thought as I did—did not know what to
make of it. . . . I remember Mother comparing
Hiawatha to Walt's, and the one seemed much the
same muddle as the other. Mother said that if
Hiawatha was poetry, perhaps Walt's was."²
Longfellow's *Hiawatha* appeared in the same year
as Walt's *Leaves of Grass*. We do not know how
highly complimented Longfellow would have felt
by Mrs. Whitman's comparison.

But the war changed for a time the themes of
Walt's compositions. He was working over his

new material, and it had in it very little about the *Children of Adam*. It would appear that when the war first broke out, Walt had some moments of exultation. It appeared to him that this was an experience that would test the old ship "Libertad" and Walt was willing the storm should break. He began a poem, but I think he did not finish it:

Welcome the storm—welcome the trial—let the waves——
Why now I shall see what the old ship is made of.
Anybody can sail with a fair wind, a smooth sea.
Come now we will see what stuff you are made of,
        Ship of Libertad.
Let others tremble and turn pale; let them ——
I want to see what ——before I die;
I welcome the menace—I welcome thee with joy.

He did not find the proper words to fill in the blanks, and as the war went on, Walt felt less defiant and more self-contained.

Sometime before 1866 when he published his *Drum-Taps,* he reviewed the year of the outbreak of the war, and its impressions upon him and his work:[3]

EIGHTEEN SIXTY-ONE

Arm'd year—year of the struggle,
No dainty rhymes or sentimental love verses for you,
        terrible year,
Not you as some pale poetling seated at a desk lisping
        cadenzas piano,

But as a strong man erect, clothed in blue clothes, advancing, carrying a rifle on your shoulder,
With well-gristled body and sunburnt face and hands,
with a knife in the belt at your side,
As I heard you shouting loud, your sonorous voice ringing
across the continent,
Your masculine voice, O year, as rising amid the great
cities,
Amid the men of Manhattan I saw you as one of the
workmen, the dwellers in Manhattan,
Or with large steps crossing the prairies out of Illinois
and Indiana,
Rapidly crossing the West with springy gait and descend-
ing the Alleghanies,
Or down from the great lakes or in Pennsylvania, or on
deck along the Ohio river,
Or southward along the Tennessee or Cumberland rivers,
or at Chattanooga on the mountain top,
Saw I your gait and saw I your sinewy limbs clothed in
blue, bearing weapons, robust year,
Heard your determin'd voice launch'd forth again and
again,
Year that suddenly sang by the mouths of the round-
lipp'd cannon,
I repeat you, hurrying, crashing, sad, distracted year.

All his life he had seen soldiers, more or less.
But what he saw in 1861 and 1862 was a vision of
another sort. In his unpublished volume, left at
home in hope of publication some day, was a poem
commenting on the contrast between soldiers as he
had seen them in times of peace, and soldiers as he
saw them now:

Forty years had I in my city seen soldiers parading,
Forty years as a pageant, till unawares the lady of this
      teeming and turbulent city,
Sleepless amid her ships, her houses, her incalculable
      wealth,
With her million children around her, suddenly,
At dead of night, at news from the south,
Incens'd struck with clinch'd hand the pavement.

A shock electric, the night sustain'd it,
Till with ominous hum our hive at daybreak pour'd out
      its myriads.
From the houses then and the workshops, and through all
      the doorways,
Leapt they tumultuous, and lo! Manhattan arming.

To the drum-taps prompt,
The young men falling in and arming,
The mechanics arming, (the trowel, the jack-plane, the
      blacksmith's hammer, tost aside with precipita-
      tion,)
The lawyer leaving his office and arming, the judge leav-
      ing the court,
The driver deserting his wagon in thè street, jumping
      down, throwing the reins abruptly down on the
      horses' backs,
The salesman leaving the store, the boss, book-keeper,
      porter, all leaving;
Squads gather everywhere by common consent and arm,
The new recruits, even boys, the old men show them how
      to wear their accoutrements, they buckle the
      straps carefully,
Outdoors arming, indoors arming, the flash of the musket-
      barrels,

The white tents cluster in camps, the arm'd sentries
      around, the sunrise cannon and again at sunset,
Arm'd regiments arrive every day, pass through the city,
      and embark from the wharves,
(How good they look as they tramp down to the river,
      sweaty, with their guns on their shoulders!
How I love them! how I could hug them, with their brown
      faces and their clothes and knapsacks cover'd
      with dust!)
The blood of the city up—arm'd! arm'd! the cry every-
      where,
The flags flung out from the steeples of churches and
      from all the public buildings and stores,
The tearful parting, the mother kisses her son, the son
      kisses his mother,
(Loth is the mother to part, yet not a word does she
      speak to detain him,)
The tumultuous escort, the ranks of policemen preceding,
      clearing the way,
The unpent enthusiasm, the wild cheers of the crowd for
      their favorites,
The artillery, the silent cannons bright as gold, drawn
      along, rumble lightly over the stones,
(Silent cannons, soon to cease your silence,
Soon unlimber'd to begin the red business;)
All the mutter of preparation, all the determin'd arming,
The hospital service, the lint, bandages and medicines,
The women volunteering for nurses, the work begun for
      in earnest, no mere parade now;
War! an arm'd race is advancing! the welcome for battle,
      no turning away;
War! be it weeks, months, or years, an arm'd race is ad-
      vancing to welcome it.

We are not informed concerning the manner in which the mother of Walt Whitman received tidings that her son George was wounded. The New York daily papers were careful to report the casualties among New York soldiers, and Walt was where newspaper information came readily to his hand. There had been scant time for a message by mail. But the letters Walt was later to write to the families of wounded men gave him a part of the material for his poem *Come up from the Fields,* and some things he remembered about the manner in which his mother received the news presumably colored the picture. Perhaps he thought out some of the lines as he was on his way to Washington, that bleak December day in 1862:

Come up from the fields, father, here's a letter from our
      Pete,
And come to the front door, mother, here's a letter from
      thy dear son.

Lo, 'tis autumn,
Lo, where the trees, deeper green, yellower and redder,
Cool and sweeten Ohio's villages with leaves fluttering in
      the moderate wind,
Where apples ripe in the orchards hang and grapes on
      the trellis'd vines,
(Smell you the smell of the grapes on the vines?
Smell you the buckwheat where the bees were lately
      buzzing?)
Above all, lo, the sky so calm, so transparent after the
      rain, and with wondrous clouds,

Below too, all calm, all vital and beautiful, and the farm
    prospers well.

Down in the fields all prospers well,
But now from the fields come, father, come at the daugh-
    ter's call,
And come to the entry, mother, to the front door come
    right away.

Fast as she can she hurries, something ominous, her steps
    trembling,
She does not tarry to smooth her hair nor adjust her cap.

Open the envelope quickly,
O this is not our son's writing, yet his name is sign'd,
O a strange hand writes for our dear son, O stricken
    mother's soul!
All swims before her eyes, flashes with black, she catches
    the main words only,
Sentences broken, *gunshot wound in the breast, cavalry
    skirmish, taken to hospital,*
At present low, but will soon be better.

Ah, now the single figure to me,
Amid all teeming and wealthy Ohio with all its cities and
    farms,
Sickly white in the face and dull in the head, very faint,
By the jamb of a door leans.

Grieve not so, dear mother, (the just-grown daughter
    speaks through her sobs,
The little sisters huddle around speechless and dismay'd,)
*See, dearest mother, the letter says Pete will soon be
    better.*

Alas, poor boy, he will never be better, (nor maybe needs
    to be better, that brave and simple soul,)
While they stand at home at the door he is dead already,
The only son is dead.

But the mother needs to be better,
She with thin form presently drest in black,
By day her meals untouch'd, then at night fitfully sleep-
    ing, often waking,
In the midnight waking, weeping, longing with one deep
    longing,
O that she might withdraw unnoticed, silent from life
    escape and withdraw
To follow, to seek, to be with her dear dead son.

The summer and autumn of 1862 had been a
time of deep searchings of heart for most men of
Walt's years. Repeated calls for troops had been
issued, and the prompt and eager response which
the first of these calls had evoked had given place
to apathy, fear and hostility. It had been necessary to resort to the draft. The terrible draft-riots
had not as yet occurred, but they were in prospect.
Able-bodied men were hastening into Canada to
escape the draft, and many who had begun pro-
ceedings for naturalization renounced their American citizenship. The passport office had to
employ extra forces of clerks to accommodate those
American citizens who had sudden and urgent
business in Europe; every vessel out of New York
would have been loaded to the Plimsol line with

them in the fall of 1862, had not the vessels been
forbidden to carry over men under sixty.[4]

In the memorandum book which Walt had in his
pocket as he rode toward Washington were many
scraps of poetry as he planned to write it. One of
these was apparently written near the end of 1862
or early in 1863, and it recorded his feelings regarding the first two years in which he had been an idle
observer of the war. It is barely possible that he
wrote them either on the train or soon after he had
taken up his residence in Washington:

QUICKSAND YEARS THAT WHIRL ME I KNOW NOT WHITHER
1861-2

Quicksand years that whirl me
    I know not whither—
Years that whirl I know not whither!
Schemes, politics fail—all is shaken—all gives way.
Only the theme I sing, the great soul,
One's self, that must never be shaken,
Out of the failures, wars, death, what at last but one's
    self is sure?
With the soul I defy you, quicksand years, slipping from
    under my feet——

Walt had not fled to Europe, still less had he
gone to the front. It was not the Quaker heritage
of the family that held him back; his brother
George had the same heritage as himself. There
were two things Walt would not do if he could
avoid it. He would not fight and he would not

work. He loved to loaf and invite his soul. He had been doing this for nearly two years since the war broke out, and he might have continued to do it if George had not been wounded. That changed everything, including the whole subsequent career of Walt Whitman.

But where was he to find George, and in what condition? And how should he proceed now that he had no money?

The slow train crept on through the short afternoon, and night fell. Cold, cramped, weary, anxious, hungry and penniless, Walt Whitman emerged from the train, and stood in the capital city of the United States.

He made his way out of the station to the spotted darkness of Pennsylvania Avenue, and looked first in this direction and then in that. Was there in Washington that night another man so unutterably alone, so disheartened, so discouraged?

There was one other man in that city as lonely and disheartened as he. On that very day, Tuesday, December 16, 1862, he said to himself, and on the following day he said to a friend, that it seemed as if God had forsaken him.[5]

The name of that other desperately lonely man was Abraham Lincoln.

II

ABRAHAM LINCOLN'S MIDNIGHT HOUR

THE night of Walt Whitman's arrival in Washington may not have been the blackest of Abraham Lincoln's many dark nights, but he was as near to despair as he ever had been in all his life. The summer and fall of 1862 had been for him one long agony. The year 1862 had begun with large promise of success for the Union Army. An obscure young officer named Ulysses S. Grant, aided by gunboats commanded by Commodore Foote, had captured Fort Henry on the Tennessee River, and the army marching across the narrow strip of land which at that point separated the Tennessee from the Cumberland, had captured Fort Donelson. This double victory, together with one that was secured by General Thomas at Mill Spring, drove the Confederate forces from Kentucky and was followed by a resolution of the Kentucky legislature assuring that state's loyalty to the Union.

A little later this same General Grant first lost and then won a battle at Shiloh, a considerable distance farther south on the Tennessee River, the most substantial victory which the Union Armies had had up to that time. A little later still the Confederate ironclad called the *Merrimac* had met in battle a curious little gunboat named the *Monitor,* and the larger and heavier ship suffered such injuries as practically to decide that the Confederate Navy would never be able to accomplish a decisive result in the War between the States.

But as the year rolled on the whole aspect changed. General Kirby Smith invaded Kentucky and utterly defeated the Union Army that disputed his progress. In the East, matters were even worse. General McClellan fought few battles and did not win any of those he fought. Out of patience with McClellan's inactivity, Lincoln removed him from the command of the Army of the Potomac. General Pope fought and lost a desperate battle. Bull Run became the scene of another and a hopeless slaughter. Washington was filled with wounded men. Three thousand Union soldiers, already there, were sent to Philadelphia and other cities in order that their cots might be used by men more recently wounded. Several of the public buildings, including the Patent Office, became hospitals. Private homes, churches, and practically all available buildings were called into requisition. From Washington went up one constant moan of pain.

General McClellan was recalled to service. He

fought at Antietam General Robert E. Lee in command of an army much smaller than his own. The battle drove Lee south from the borders of Maryland, but it was a very meager victory for McClellan. With two Confederate armies, one in Kentucky threatening Louisville and Cincinnati, and the other in Maryland threatening Baltimore and Washington, the late summer and early autumn drove the North almost to panic. Enlistments almost ceased and even the draft failed to bring in the requisite number of soldiers.

After the battle of Antietam, President Lincoln issued his proclamation promising freedom to the slaves in those states and parts of states under rebellion on the first of January, 1863. In the main, his proclamation was received coldly. He lost some of his best friends on account of it, and he did not gain the hearty support of the abolitionists. He issued his proclamation as he told his Cabinet because he had promised God that he would do so, but no blessing appeared to come from God as the result of it.

The November elections were disastrous for Lincoln. New York, New Jersey, Pennsylvania, Delaware, Ohio, Indiana and Illinois all went against the party on which Lincoln depended for his support in the two Houses of Congress. Such a series of sorrows and disappointments never came in succession to any one President of the United States as came to Abraham Lincoln in the latter months of 1862.

Disappointed again at General McClellan's inactivity, Lincoln removed him from command of
the Army of the Potomac on November seventh.
In McClellan's place, Lincoln appointed General
Ambrose E. Burnside, whose handsome side-
whiskers furnished a name for his then fashionable
style of beard. No charge of timidity could be
brought against Burnside. He found his army
encamped in and about Falmouth on the northern
bank of the Rappahannock River opposite the town
of Fredericksburg. On the seventh of November,
there were piled behind his headquarters, the Lacy
house, a fine old southern mansion, materials
for two pontoon bridges, each four hundred
and fifty feet long.[1] His engineers informed
him that they had crossed by night and explored
the ground on the other side and thought it unwise
to erect the bridges above the town because there
were no convenient roads on the other side of the
river, but that there was a place a few miles below
where the bridges could be erected and the army
safely transported across out of range of the Confederate guns. But the army did not move for
nearly a month and by that time General Robert
E. Lee himself had come up with large reinforce-
ments and had fortified Fredericksburg and the
range of hills behind it known by the name of
Marye's Heights.

On Saturday, December thirteenth, General
Burnside, disregarding the recommendations of his
engineers, fought this battle. He caused one of his

bridges to be erected directly into the town of
Fredericksburg, and the other only two miles
below. Of all battles bravely fought but unwisely
planned, the battle of Fredericksburg was among
the very worst. It involved a frontal attack upon
a fortified elevation, where soldiers stood four and
five deep behind stone walls. That any men in
the Union Army should have advanced against
that wall and lived to get back across one or the
other of the pontoon bridges, would seem to prove
that the day of miracles was not wholly past. The
Federal loss was 12,800 men, and Lee lost 4,300.
The bleeding and disorganized ranks of the Union
Army broke into fragments and those who could
do so found their way back to the north side of the
swift and deep Rappahannock.

All day Sunday and Monday the appalling news
was coming into Washington, with long lines of
ambulances from the boat landing, bringing thousands of wounded men. The horror of it sickened
the national capital and settled upon it in a cloud
of impenetrable gloom. On Tuesday the Senate
met, but it had no heart to do business. It
adjourned promptly in order that the Republican
majority might send the Democratic minority beyond hearing distance, while the Republicans
gathered to consider the horrible situation. Of
everything else they were uncertain, except this,
that the man to blame for all their misfortune was
Abraham Lincoln. Comforted by the fact that no

Democrats were where they could hear, the Republican senators poured out the vials of their wrath upon the head of the President. At the other end of Pennsylvania Avenue, in an upper room of the White House, sunk in the very blackness of despair, Abraham Lincoln sat alone. He was there on that night when Walt Whitman reached Washington. Walt was lonely and friendless, but not so lonely or so friendless as Abraham Lincoln.

On the following night which was Wednesday, the Republican caucus of the Senate sent a committee practically demanding that the President should resign. What they asked was that he should appoint a new Cabinet virtually of the Senate's selection. That was the night Abraham Lincoln told his friends it seemed as if God has forsaken him.[2] How Abraham Lincoln met that crisis and gained mastery of himself and of his Cabinet and of the Senate, need not here and now be told. All these things he did in the closing days of December, 1862.[3]

The first of January came—the day on which he had promised to issue the final proclamation which guaranteed the freedom of the slaves. That was the day of the President's formal reception, and all that morning he was shaking hands with the curious crowds that trod the White House carpets and walked away to tell their friends that they had had what some of them thought was the doubtful honor of shaking hands with President Lincoln.

It was late in the afternoon when Secretary William H. Stewart and his son and Assistant, Frederick, brought to the President the engrossed parchment of the Emancipation Proclamation. Lincoln dipped his pen in the ink and paused. He could hardly hold the pen. Waiting until he could control the muscles of his hand, he said, "I never in my life felt more certain that I was doing right than I do in the signing of this paper. But I have been receiving calls and shaking hands since eleven o'clock this morning until my arm is stiff and numb. Now, this signature will be closely examined, and if they find my hand trembled, they will say, 'He had some compunction.' But, anyway, it is going to be done."

Then carefully, so as to remove anything that could be made to appear like a trembling and uncertain signature, Abraham Lincoln signed the Proclamation that freed the slaves.

III

WALT WHITMAN VISITS THE ARMY

When Walt Whitman arrived in Washington that Tuesday night in December, 1862, he first made inquiry as to the location of No. 394 L Street near Fourteenth. He had no money to pay his fare on the horse-cars, but he was strong and able to walk. Rather late in the evening he arrived.

William Douglas O'Connor was a big, handsome and generous Irishman who had been a reporter on a Boston paper. He was a hot abolitionist and at the time of the John Brown raid his outspoken utterances in favor of that hero brought him into criticism. His views were too radical for even the Boston papers, and he found himself out of employment. He tried his hand at a novel entitled *Harrington*.

His publishers were Thayer and Eldridge, the same who published the third edition of *Leaves of Grass*. It was on Walt's first visit to Boston in 1860, in connection with the publication of his own book, that he met O'Connor. The two authors were about equally unsuccessful so far as Thayer and Eldridge were concerned; they had this in common that they contributed in about equal measure to the bankruptcy of that firm. O'Connor's radical opinions on the negro question and Whitman's frankness on the sex problem, were both displeasing to the publishers' constituency. Charles W. Eldridge, the junior partner in the publishing firm, sought a clerkship in Washington, and found it in the office of the paymaster.

O'Connor was fortunate in obtaining a clerkship in the lighthouse division. There were few things O'Connor loved better than fighting. If he had been unmarried, he might have gone to war. He was not interested in a war to save the Union, but was very greatly interested in a war to end slavery. Whitman, on the contrary, believed in the Union as a symbol of American vastness and unity but was not, at this time, a very enthusiastic friend of the slaves.

Whitman knew that O'Connor was in Washington and had his address. To his hospitable home Walt wended his way that winter night, and the door swung wide open with generous welcome. O'Connor's wife was a lovely and cultured and hospitable woman. O'Connor, poor as he was, had a generous heart. In a little room at the top of the O'Connor home, Walt slept on Tuesday, Wednesday and Thursday nights.

The Washington daily papers carried lists of the war hospitals within the city. There were twenty-six of them, in churches, halls and Government buildings. Information was given as to the most convenient ways of getting to these several places, for there were many people in Washington on errands like that of Walt.

On Wednesday and Thursday Walt tramped the rounds of the Washington hospitals. He was one of a long procession that thronged the streets of Washington after Fredericksburg, as similar crowds arrived after each of the important eastern battles. The hospitals equipped themselves for the meeting of these inquirers. A list of all wounded men was kept at the entrance so that inquiring friends might be informed with the least possible delay to themselves, and the least disturbance to the hospital, whether a particular soldier was within. In those two days, Walt made the rounds of practically all the hospitals in Washington. He satisfied himself that his brother George was not there.

Those two days, however, were not lost to Walt in his subsequent literary work. When, in after years, he told of his hospital experience in the Civil War, he spoke of it as belonging to the years 1862, 1863, 1864 and 1865. Those two days were the 1862 part of his hospital experience.

O'Connor and his wife were a great source of comfort to Walt at this time. O'Connor had very little money but he was able to make a small loan, enough to provide Walt against desperate need.

He remarked genially that a pickpocket who could not rob Walt would not be worthy of a respectable place in his profession. The fact that Walt did not find his brother George in Washington meant one of three things: that his wound was fatal and he had died, that he was too badly wounded to be moved, or that his wound was not serious and he was on the way to recovery. In any event, Walt's next place of inquiry was in the general region of Fredericksburg. O'Connor helped Walt to secure a pass to Falmouth and back. This involved his taking a boat to Aquia Creek landing and a train from there, a matter of ten or twelve miles, to Falmouth. Both the boat and the railroad were under government control. Thus it came about that on Friday evening, December nineteenth, Walt Whitman reached Falmouth, and in due time found the camp of the Fifty-first New York.

George Washington Whitman did not give Walt a very hearty welcome. His wound had been trivial. He was up and around and back on duty, able to look after himself, and not at all certain that Walt would have been any great help to him if he had been sick. However, Walt was there and there was no particular reason why he should not remain for a few days if he wanted to do so.

Walt certainly wanted to remain. The habit of the newspaper reporter was upon him, and he thought he might get some good copy, so he remained for a week and one day. It was for him a

care-free and happy experience. The memories of
the battle had already receded and taken their place
in the minds of the soldiers with the other battles
which they had fought and lost. The battle had
been followed by heavy rain and severe cold, but
that was past. During the eight days of Walt's
stay the sun shone, and while it was undeniably
December, the days were comfortably warm. The
soldiers had extemporized fireplaces and had practically gone into winter quarters. They had plenty
of food and very good food at that. Around the
fire at night they sang in cheerful expectation:

I'll eat when I'm hungry and drink when I'm dry,
And if the Johnnies don't kill me, I'll live till I die.

That kind of a song pleased Walt. With his
brother George he seems to have had very little to
do, but his brother's rank gave Walt a place in an
officer's tent, and what was equally important, a
seat in the officers' mess. Walt kept a diary by fits
and starts. He never maintained that or any other
orderly method a great while at a time, but on Sunday he began to make a record of his adventures.
His original record is in the Library of Congress.[1]

This is the way his record began:

Friday, Saturday and Sunday, Dec. 19, 20 and 21, was
at Falmouth, opposite Fredericksburg. The grub was
good. Had a tip-top time every way. Capt. Sims, Frank
Butler, Orderly McReady and —— all well. Grub good.

Walt left a blank for the name of the fifth occupant of the tent in which he slept, and he did not later record it. The name was certainly not that of Walt's brother George, who was disgusted to have Walt there. Walt's letter to his mother, written after his return to Washington, gives her reassuring news of George, but his note-books do not mention the brother whom he had gone to the front to find.

Walt's chief interest during that sojourn at Falmouth, aside from his three meals at the warmth of the campfire, was in visiting among the men of his brother's regiment and those of another regiment in the same brigade, and making notes of incidents and experiences which he might possibly use later in some of his writings. Apparently he did not go inside the hospital. He found the soldiers communicative, and he compiled what amounted to an outline of the history of his brother's regiment. He used this some months later in one of his newspaper articles.

Sunday, December twenty-first, was a mild and beautiful day. The regiments were assembled on parade, and Walt was present at the review. The sight made a deep impression upon him. War, as he beheld it, did not appear very terrible. On the day after Christmas, he had his one recorded contact, during this visit, with the grim side of war. He saw three dead men covered with blankets lying outside the brigade hospital, and later walking in the open field, by mere chance he came upon a squad of soldiers burying the dead, probably these same three dead soldiers. It lacked one day of being two weeks since the battle. The daily death-rate in any one regimental or brigade hospital was not large. There was, however, a row of graves of soldiers from that same group who had died during the preceding two weeks. His record is important and must be given complete:[2]

Friday Dec. 26.

Early this morning I walked out in the open fields, one side of the camp. I found some of the soldiers digging graves. There were for the 51st, N. Y. and 11th, N. H. There was a row of graves there already, each with a slat of board, generally a barrel-head on which was inscribed the name of the soldier. Death is nothing here: as you step out in the morning from your tent you see on a stretcher a shapeless object extended over which is thrown a dark green blanket—the covering of some wounded sick soldier who died in the hospital tent during the night. Perhaps there is a row of three or four of these. . . . There is a detail of men to bury them; all useless ceremony is omitted. The stern realities of a long campaign make the old etiquette a cumber and nuisance.

Walt spent but one day after this at Falmouth. On Sunday morning, December twenty-eighth, he took train for Aquia Creek, connecting with the boat which brought him back to Washington late that afternoon.

It is interesting to remind ourselves that if he had waited a few days longer, he might have seen

at Falmouth President and Mrs. Abraham
Lincoln. The President went down to look over
the battle-field, to gain knowledge if he could by an
inspection of the field and conference with the
commanding general. As a result of that visit and
of what he learned otherwise, he removed General
Burnside from command, and appointed in his
place General Joseph Hooker whom the soldiers
called "Fighting Joe."

It is pleasant to know that not only Walt Whitman but Abraham Lincoln moved about Falmouth
with some measure of relief from care. One little
incident is of record which deserves the tribute of
a passing smile. As President and Mrs. Lincoln
were driving about the fringes of the camps, they
came upon a crowd of contrabands. Not only
negro men but women and children were huddled
under the shelter of the army and depending upon
it for rations. They seemed to have no care on
earth. The little colored children were running
around nearly naked and quite happy. Mrs.
Lincoln pointed to a group of these, and address-
ing her husband asked, "How many of those little
pickaninnies do you suppose are named for you?"
He recalled that he had been nominated about two
years and a half before, and he answered her cheer-
fully that he imagined about fifty per cent. of those
who were two and a half years old or less, shared
with him the honor of the name of Abraham
Lincoln.

Walt Whitman left Falmouth before Lincoln came. There were some wounded men on the boat. Most, if not all of these, were recovering. It was no longer necessary to move dangerously sick men from the field hospitals. It is not impossible of course that one of them died on the boat as Walt afterward thought he remembered, but most that he later recalled as having occurred on that day must have been colored by his imagination.

And now we face the fact that our material for an authentic record of Walt Whitman's experiences is more limited than any of his biographers have assumed.[3] Even his records that were later published as having been made at the time and on the spot of the adventures recorded have been so edited and revised and enlarged by Walt that we do not know how much they should be discounted. The notes he made from day to day while he was near Falmouth, appear to cover pretty fully the entire time of his visit. For all practical purposes, they are an adequate record of what he saw and did, but when he got back to Washington and told his friends about it details began to change. The mild weather gave place to stormy days and freezing nights. The "good grub" which he so enjoyed, gave place to hard army rations, heroically endured. The three dead soldiers whom he saw buried by a squad detailed for the purpose, became a much larger number, and, what is more important, it was no other than Walt Whitman himself who had charge of the burial. As years went by, it was easy for him to remember that he was in charge of that boat-load of wounded soldiers going back to Washington. We need not here and now reprint these stories as he later told them, either with or without the needless further exaggerations of the biographers. It is enough that we compare with the foregoing account made at the time, Walt's first revision of his experience. Instead of eight days, he had been at the front "a good part of the winter." He was there at the time of the battle and was on the battle-field among the wounded, ministering to them. On the day following the battle he went out under a flag of truce to direct the burial of the dead. Wearied at night by these strenuous exertions, he wrapped himself in his blanket and lay down in the mud, having welcomed his salt pork and hardtack. This letter was written from Washington, March 19, 1863. A short quotation will suffice:

Dear Nat and Fred Gray:

Since I left New York I was down in the Army of the Potomac in front with my brother a good part of the winter, commencing time of the battle of Fredericksburg—have seen *war-life*, the real article—folded myself in a blanket, lying down in the mud with composure, relished salt pork and hardtack—have been on the battle-field among the wounded, the faint and the bleeding, to give them nourishment—have gone over with a flag of truce the next day to help direct the burial of the

dead. . . . I spent the Christmas holidays on the
Rappahannock. During January came up hither, took
a lodging room here.[4]

A little later he told of having served as a nurse
in the Lacy house, and of his seeing a cart-load of
arms, legs, hands and feet piled up outside of it.
He saw nothing of the kind. He was not in the
Lacy house. He heard soldiers tell that they had
seen on the day after the battle these and other
gruesome sights, and he took over their experiences
as his own.[5]

On Monday, Walt wrote to his mother, his letters
to whom are among the best of his writings, and
show his character in some of its finest traits. He
was concerned to relieve her anxiety concerning
George, and he did so. He gave her a cheerful
account of his adventures and told her of his purpose to remain for the present in Washington, and
to secure employment if he could. We are quite
certain he did not attend President Lincoln's New
Year's reception, although the public was welcome.
His strong grip had no part in the wearying of the
President's arm on the day on which he signed the
final Proclamation of Emancipation. He was
chiefly employed in looking for a job.

Not only had Walt seen no fighting during his
week at Falmouth, but he had not been very near
to where any fighting had been done. While he
mixed the notes of his own personal experience with

the tales that were told to him, it is fairly easy to separate the two. His descriptions of the scenes which he actually observed are all of the rear and of the camp. But he had the real gift of the journalist in visualizing what was related to him. He began work on a poem descriptive of a battle. I copy from his note-book this vivid description, disjointed and incomplete as he left it there:

A Battle

(scenes, sounds &c)

The opening of the fight when the skirmishing begins, the
 irregular snap, snap
The wild excitement and delight infernal,
The position of the dead. Some with arms raised, poised
 in the air.
Some lying on the ground, the dead in every position.
One reached forward with finger extended, pointing—
 one in the position of firing.
(Some of the dead, how soon they turn black in the face
 and swollen!)
The scene at the batteries—what crashing and smoking!
 How proud the men are of their pieces!)
The varied sounds of the different missiles—the short s-s-t
 of the rifled ball
The shells exploded leaving a small white cloud,
The haze and buzz of the great shells
The grape like the rushing whirr of wind
The continual rattle of musketry never intermitted from
 the other side.
The short th-h-t, th-h-t, th-h-t with irregular intervals
 between

The peculiar shriek of certain shells—the thud of the
    round balls falling in the soft earth,
The shouts and curses of men—the orders for the officers
The wild cry of a regiment charging, the Colonel with his
    unsheathed sword,
The gaps cut in the enemies' batteries (quickly fill'd up,
    no delay)
The groans of the wounded, the sight of blood.
Sometimes the curious lull for a few, serious awful quiet
    moments, no firing on either side.
The [n] resumed again, the noise worse than ever—
All of a sudden from our part of the line, a Cheer for a
    fine mount, or charge, Spirited attack
The chief-gunner ranges and sights his piece, and selects
    a fuse of the right time.
(After a shot see how he leans aside and looks eagerly off,
    to see the effect!)
Then after the battle what a scene!
The wounded, the surgeons and ambulances—
O the hideous damned, horrid hell of war; were the
    preachers preaching of hell?
O there is no hell more damned than this hell of war!
O the beautiful young men!
O the beautiful clotted hair! the faces!
Some lie on their backs with faces up of arms extended—

But as Walt settled down to life in Washington
he found some experiences less grewsome to write
about. Here is a poem he penciled in the book he
was carrying at this time:

The Soul Reaching Throughout for Love

As the spider from some little promontory, throwing out
    filament after filament tireless out of itself, that

one at least may catch and form a link, a bridge,
a connection,
As the—the—

O I saw one passing alone, saying hardly a word—yet
full of love I detected him by certain signs—
O Eyes ever wistfully turning! O silent eyes!
O the latent oceans, the fathomless oceans of love!
O waiting oceans of love! the yearning and fervent sweat
of your sweet souls!
But Dead, unknown on this earth, the future delicious and
long; here unspoken, never born!
You fathomless souls of love—you pent and unknown
oceans of love!

Washington did not know it, but Walt Whitman had arrived. He was a tall, hairy, robust man, with hair already white and full beard turning gray. On his arrival he stood six feet in stature, and weighed one hundred and ninety-six pounds. Before long, he gained weight to two hundred and ten.[6] He was in the best of health, but it would have been better for him, physically and in every way, if he had trained himself down to one hundred and eighty. His flesh was pink, soft, womanish. He was not muscular, for he shrank from heavy exercise. He stood erect and carried himself well. He had no lack of self-confidence, and seemed abundantly capable of taking care of himself. His mind was completely free from all anxiety about his brother George, and

George was glad to have Walt away from camp where he had no responsibility for him. Walt had two concerns. One was to find a publisher for his forthcoming book; the other and pressing need was to find some position in Washington which would enable him to stay there and obtain a living without working or fighting. Unfortunately for him, there were large numbers of partly disabled men seeking work in Washington, and there was a prejudice against providing positions for able-bodied men who were capable of carrying muskets and who wanted to do work that could be done by women or by men who had been wounded in the service of their country. This was the competition which Walt Whitman faced in fear. Apart from that, he had few cares.

IV

"THE WOUND-DRESSER"

William Douglas O'Connor was a friend in need. He and Walt went together to the paymaster's department and found their friend Eldridge. As Walt and O'Connor had helped to put Eldridge in his clerical position by assisting in making his firm in Boston bankrupt, and as one good turn deserved another, they looked at him now to help find work for Walt. Eldridge proved equal to the emergency. He introduced Walt to Major Hapgood, head of his department, and Hapgood provided Walt with part-time work. There was not enough of it to occupy his full time, and while it did not pay very well it provided Walt with daily bread and left him a large amount of free time for such occupations as he enjoyed.

The O'Connors were not in a position to give Walt a permanent room in their home. He continued to take many of his meals there, but as soon as he was earning money, he had to secure a room. He found it on the third floor back in a tumble-down tenement at the corner of Sixth and E

Streets. It was a poor old building but it stood diagonally across from the home of Secretary Chase. Walt began immediately securing from his literary friends recommendations that might help him to a position. The first of these was from Ralph Waldo Emerson, and the next was from John T. Trowbridge.

Trowbridge visited Washington and was a guest of Secretary Chase. He proposed to call on Walt. "Don't come before ten o'clock," ordered Walt. Trowbridge timed his visit accordingly, but was still more than sufficiently early. He found Walt in what Trowbridge called a "terrible room." Walt was partly dressed and had a small fire and was cutting slices of bread from a baker's loaf with his jack-knife. His cupboard was an oblong box in which he set parcels of cheese, butter and sugar as they came from the grocery. He had a tiny tea-kettle and a covered tin cup he used as a teapot. He also had a bowl and one spoon. These articles comprised his entire housekeeping outfit. Walt was unabashed by his own appearance and that of his room. He toasted his bread on the end of a splinter. His plates were pieces of brown paper, which he burned after using, finding that to be the most expeditious way of washing his dishes. Trowbridge has preserved for us this little picture of Walt's housekeeping. As to how clean Walt was in his own person, there is divergence of testimony.

The presence in Washington of so many

wounded men made it necessary to have a large corps of volunteer nurses. Early in the war, Secretary Stanton placed Miss Dorothea Dix in charge of all the women nurses of the army. At the outset also Clara Barton established her organization whose distinctive work was the immediate relief of the wounded through field hospitals in immediate proximity to the firing line. But the very large base hospitals in and about Washington called for help beyond these organized provisions. It is sad to confess that most of this volunteer help was worse than useless. The Reverend Doctor Bellows, at the head of the largest organization for the relief of the wounded, brought in a sweeping indictment against the inefficiency of most of the women nurses.

As for the men nurses, we have a sad exhibit in that which happened after the second battle of Bull Run. A mob of volunteers, estimated at one thousand, left by government train and in two hundred vehicles, for the battle front. It had been particularly requested that each nurse should bring a supply of brandy. Not much of the brandy and not many of the nurses reached the front, and most of those who did arrive were ignominiously sent back.

In Washington it was not so bad. Hospitals there were under supervision, and the sentimental and incompetent nurses were weeded out in part at least. Hundreds of Washington's best people devoted themselves earnestly to hospital work, some to nursing and others to visiting the sick. Foremost among the agencies which undertook this work were the Sanitary Commission and the Christian Commission. Neither of these organizations undertook to supply nurses. For that matter, Dorothea Dix would brook no interference with her selection and control of the nurses. The Sanitary Commission provided hospital equipment, lint, bandages, jellies and fruit, especially lemons. The Christian Commission did not undertake either nursing or food or medicine. Its workers, who were called "delegates," were instructed to give personal service. Each delegate was furnished a book for notes and records, and in its forefront were nine closely printed pages of very sensible instructions. The delegates were not to interfere with the work of chaplains, physicians or nurses. They were not to force religion upon reluctant men. They were to go as representatives of a religious organization, but they were to go as friends. If men wanted religious help, and there was a shortage of chaplains, the delegates were to read the Bible if requested, and on occasion, to offer prayer, but these ministrations were not to be obtrusive. The delegates were to write letters, distribute newspapers and other good reading matter, provide envelopes, stamps and letter-paper, and to give comfort and cheer without interfering with any one.

Strangely, we find Walt Whitman soon after his arrival in Washington, accredited as a delegate of the United States Christian Commission. That organization furnished him with a good Morocco bound book stamped with the style of the commission and with his name, and he on the inside, proudly wrote, "Walt Whitman, Soldiers' Missionary to Hospital, Camp, and Battlefield."[1]

That title is interesting for more than one reason. There were three distinct kinds of "Delegates" of the Christian Commission, and their duties were carefully differentiated in the book of instructions. One was for service in camp, one was for ministrations on the battle-field, and the third was for friendly visitation in hospitals. There was nothing small about Walt. He appropriated immediately all three.

The nine pages of Instructions to delegates were followed by two pages of "General Suggestions." As showing the spirit of the organization under which Walt worked, I copy these two pages from Walt's own book:

General Suggestions

As the Christian Commission aims to appoint Christian gentlemen as delegates, any suggestions about personal deportment may be superfluous. They understand perfectly well that their work is that of aiding others, not dictating to them. Officers are supreme in the field, and Surgeons in the hospital and on the battle ground. All others coming to their aid should hold themselves subject to orders, and place themselves under orders, and then do with their might, whatever work their hands find to do, commending themselves to God and their own consciences, and to officers and surgeons by the wisdom, energy and efficiency of their service, and by their gentlemanly Christian courtesy to all. Each one should be provided with a pocket memorandum book and pencil, and use them freely in noting facts, names, incidents, dates, and everything of interest. Also, with paper, pen, ink, envelopes and stamps, for his own use as well as to give to those who need them. *He should report his work often to the office of the Christian Commission, with facts and incidents for publication;* and immediately upon his return from the work, he should report the fact to this office, in person or by letter, in order that the proper record may be made on the books of the Commission.

All faithful chaplains should be sought out and aided as far as possible, and informed that by written application to this office, aid of almost any kind for their work, could be obtained and sent to them free of expense.

The circular of the Christian Commission to chaplains and working Christians in the army, should be placed in the hands, or sent to as many as possible, of those for whom it is designed.

And finally, this whole work in any and every department, should be pushed with Christ-like earnestness. "Work while it is day;" the words of Jesus when about to open the eyes of the blind man found by his wayside, or those other words of his childhood, characteristic of His whole life: "Wist ye not, I must be about my Father's business," should be our watch-words. The wounded and sick in the hospital will soon pass away to the army, or the home, or the judgment—the living in the camp of to-day, may to-morrow be hastened away to the field of carnage.

What we do must be done quickly; even so let us do. Amen.

> *By order of the Christian Commission.*
>
> GEO. H. STUART,
>
> *Chairman.*

PHILADELPHIA, *September 15th*, 1862.

It was thoroughly characteristic of Walt, and not wholly to his credit, that in all that he was later to write about his hospital work, he never, so far as I am aware, gave any public recognition to the organization which supported him in his beginnings of it.

Sometime in the spring of 1863, Walt passed a stationery store where unsold diaries of 1862 were offered for sale at a bargain price. One of these diaries he bought. He went through the book and leaving the days of the week as they were, changed the numerals of days of the month. His first entry was Thursday, April 16, 1863, which was probably the day he bought the book. He kept that diary perhaps longer than he had ever succeeded in maintaining one. It is that book which comes nearest to showing us how he actually spent his time. Apparently, he devoted to his work of hospital visitation his Sundays and about three afternoons a week. We have no reason to suppose that at any time he averaged more than this.

Just how long he remained in the employ of the Christian Commission we do not know. His pay was presumably very small, but the delegates were

supposed to be paid. We do not know why he gave
up this work. We might hazard a conjecture that
it did not remain satisfactory to either side for a
very great length of time. We can scarcely
imagine that Walt would permanently have enjoyed work for such an organization—neither can
we believe that his irresponsibility and irregularity
in the matter of times and services would be
permanently acceptable. There was, however, no
unhappy parting. Walt himself has assured us
that he did not shrink from reading the Bible to the
sick or even offering prayer if a dying man asked
him to do so. He himself published to the world
that he was not only not ashamed but very proud
of having done so. He left on record no complaint
against the Christian Commission for requiring of
him any service that violated his conscience. On
the other hand, it is not at all likely that the
Christian Commission was much concerned over
Walt's lack of orthodoxy or that it ever disturbed
itself by an effort to find out whether he was ortho-
dox or not. Not even Walt's most devoted friends
have ever howled to high Heaven in protest against
the Christian Commission for discharging that use-
ful heretic Walt Whitman.

Walt could have recorded, without any loss of
self-respect, that he worked for a time as the accredited representative of a religious organization.
There was nothing in the relation of that association that forced him into any attitude of incon-

sistency. He did not need to pretend that he was any more religious than he was. And we should really like to know just how the arrangement worked. He ought to have told us. He ate the bread of the Christian Commission, found through that organization the means and the method of hospital visitation, and for every reason of honor should have related in his reminiscences "written on the spot" how long he did that work and when and why he left it for work of his own, similar but independent. We can not regret that he emerged into a work of his own; it was doubtless better that he did so. But a man who told so many times what professed to be the full story of his hospital work should have given us the full narrative. I judge that in the light of such religion or lack of it as he professed, he was ashamed to tell that he had worked for a religious organization, and, that, boastful of his independence, he was reluctant to tell how much he learned from the Christian Commission. But he was not ashamed to have read the Bible and to have offered prayer in the hospitals, and he was not ashamed to have eaten the bread of the organization whose name he carefully kept out of his own story of those interesting days.

We may venture one other conjecture, which is that Walt, being a newspaper man, discovered very early that his own articles in the New York and Brooklyn papers would bring him sufficient money for all needs of this character.[2] Such letters he wrote. His mother, and other members of his family, sent him small sums. Ralph Waldo Emerson sent him a few dollars. A good many people sent him a dollar each. I have reckoned his receipts from his most lucrative articles and they appear to total about ninety-one dollars. But there could be few tasks so unprofitable as an auditing of his books. Walt was no bookkeeper. We have no reason to suppose that he misappropriated any money sent him. We have quite as little reason to suppose that he found it necessary to give any money of his own. It was not incumbent upon him to give money. He did not have it to give, but he had given what was much more valuable, sympathy and service. Certain of Walt's biographers have made the most wild and extravagant estimates as to the thousands of dollars which Walt solicited and the other thousands which he gave. If his total receipts and expenditures ever reached one thousand dollars or any sum approaching it, I have found no record of it in the books he kept. Large sums were not necessary. What he gave to a sick soldier was the daily paper, a sweet cracker, an apple, a sheet of writing paper and a stamped envelope, or to save even this small expenditure in part, a sheet of paper and an envelope franked by some member of Congress. In exceptional cases, he gave very small sums of money, ten cents or twenty-five cents. This was exactly what he was instructed to do, and just what he should have done. He did not need much money, and he probably used what money he had with quite sufficient wisdom.

He never was a "wound-dresser"[3] in any professional way. A strong man such as he could not be about the hospitals as much as he was without being called occasionally to help in the dressing of a wound or the lifting of a patient. We have no reason to doubt that Walt did this frequently, willingly and effectively. But this was only incidental. The Christian Commission employed him to be a helper and a friend. When he worked independently he followed much the same line. He has told us in detail so much about his ministrations we are in no great doubt as to their character and extent. Some days he would go through a whole ward, or more than one, with a stamped envelope or a piece of fruit for practically every patient. Some days he would spend practically the whole afternoon with a single patient who particularly needed him. We have good reason to believe that he did this work well.

We do not need the extravagant stories about many a man almost dead of whom the doctors said, "Turn him over to Whitman," and whose recovery was thenceforth assured. No one was turned over to Whitman in that way, but a great many men were cheered and comforted by him. His service did not differ in character from that of innumerable other volunteers, nor are we certain that his exceeded all others in extent. We know very well that he did not permit the sick and wounded to take up all his time. He found a good deal of time for the expression of his friendship with other men, and more than enough time for association with the kind of women of whom Washington at that time was full, and very little to his profit.

As a sample of what uninformed admirers of Whitman have written, we may quote from James Thomson, the English poet, a single paragraph:

I am informed that it was through Emerson's introduction that he obtained the sanction of President Lincoln for this purpose of charity, with authority to draw the ordinary army rations, Whitman stipulating at the same time that he would not receive any remuneration for his services.

This is as nearly wrong in every word and syllable as such a paragraph could be. Emerson never introduced Whitman to Lincoln. Lincoln was never called upon for any sanction of Whitman's work, nor was it necessary. Whitman did not draw army rations nor any rations accruing to him out of his hospital work. He depended upon his own efforts for board as did the other volunteer workers. But least true of all the foregoing statements, is that Whitman stipulated that he should not receive remuneration for his services. Never in all his life did Whitman stipulate that he should not be paid if he had opportunity to collect pay.

His pay from the Christian Commission was small. His pay as a volunteer worker was nothing. But when Walt could get any pay he took it.

Most of Walt's biographers go far out of their way to make it apparent that Walt in declining to enlist was motivated by the conviction that he could render larger service in the hospitals. Dr. R. M. Bucke may speak for them:

Those who joined the ranks and fought the battles of the Republic did well; but when the world knows, as it is beginning to know, how this man, without any encouragement from without, under no compulsion, simply without beat of drum or any cheers of approval, went down into those immense lazar houses and devoted his days and nights, his heart and soul, and at last his life and health, to America's sick and wounded sons, it will say that he did even better.

A man is not to be condemned for not enlisting as a soldier. Many brave and patriotic men find larger and equally self-denying service in other and for them more important fields. But it is not honest to pretend that Walt stayed out of the army for the sake of nursing sick soldiers. He remained in Brooklyn, drinking beer at Pfaff's, leading an idle and very free life for nearly the entire first half of the war. He remained in Washington in the hope of securing employment with a minimum of labor. Being there, he gave an unknown and vastly overestimated but still very considerable portion of his time to hospital visitation. For so much he deserved full credit. But even here it is to be remembered that his only possible hope of securing a government clerkship was on the plea that he was rendering important free hospital service.

On October 1, 1863, Walt developed a new kind of service. On that day, as he recorded in his diary, he "commenced reading pieces" to sick soldiers. Presumably some of these pieces were his own poems. One would give a good deal to know which ones he read and how the soldiers enjoyed them. John T. Trowbridge, who came nearer than any other friend of Whitman to learning the facts about his work, said that some of the soldiers did not like Walt, that they could not understand him and thought his performances stupid and uninteresting. These, however, appear to have been in the minority. Whitman, living near at hand, having abundant time to give, and with no home responsibilities, distributed his fruit, papers, tracts and postage stamps and wrote letters and "read pieces." He gave personal friendship and sympathy. Hundreds of men in army hospitals died of sheer homesickness. We can believe that Walt gave his sick friends what they most needed.

Twice in the spring of 1864, Walt secured military passes to go, once to Arlington and once to Alexandria, "on business." Whether this business had anything to do with his hospital work, we do not know. Each was a single-trip pass. It is quite possible that he went once to Alexandria and once to Arlington to visit some particular soldier whom he knew to be sick there, but mainly he was at the Armory Hospital in Washington or in one of the other hospitals close at hand. For this service, he had no pass and he needed none.[4]

In February, 1864, Walt made his second and last visit to the army. The headquarters was then at Culpeper. He went with his friend, Major Hapgood, the paymaster who had an official errand and took Walt along, possibly in the capacity of a guard. Walt was there several days and visited some field hospitals and distributed small gifts that he had taken with him for the purpose. He returned to Washington, obtaining only part-time work but still endeavoring to obtain a permanent position. His work gave him a bare living and no promise for the future.

John T. Trowbridge, in a personal visit in the home of Secretary Chase, tried to secure a permanent clerkship for Walt, and to this end handed Chase a letter from Ralph Waldo Emerson, supporting the request. Chase was glad to have Emerson's autograph but not at all interested in securing a clerkship for an able-bodied man who would not fight and who besides was understood to be the author of a rather vulgar book. Walt had a letter also to Charles Sumner, but he did not find opportunity to present it, and it is not at all likely that it would have done him any good.

In June, 1864, Walt's health broke. Certainly his hospital work had not done his health any good but we know enough about his habits of living and diet to assure ourselves that the hospitals may not have been wholly responsible. In that month he returned to Brooklyn, and it is generally believed that he remained at home six months. That, however, is not the case. He returned to Washington early in the fall and was there in October, 1864. John Hay, Junior Secretary to President Lincoln, was an admirer of Walt, and twice or more obtained free passes for him to go to Brooklyn and back. The one which he secured in October, 1864, was obtained in order that Walt might go to Brooklyn and use his influence among his friends to promote the reelection of Lincoln. Walt remained in Brooklyn until the end of January, 1865. In good measure he recovered his strength, but he never was quite so vigorous as he had previously been. During his vacation he worked on his book *Drum-Taps*. Then he returned to Washington more eager than ever to secure a permanent position. The war was nearing its end. When it was over, thousands of discharged soldiers would be clamoring for clerical positions. They would be able to say, and did say, that they had lost their previous positions by fighting for their country and that they were physically unfit for heavy work. If Walt got a job in Washington he had need to make haste.

V

A POET SEEKING A PUBLISHER

ABRAHAM LINCOLN and Walt Whitman lived in Washington, and not very far apart, from the night of Sunday, December 28, 1862, until the death of Abraham Lincoln on the morning of Saturday, April 15, 1865. The last year of this period was broken for Walt by several absences in Brooklyn. Walt's first pass secured by John Hay at the request of O'Connor, October 9, 1863, took Walt to Brooklyn for rather more than two months. He was absent for three other extended periods. In the latter days of his war-time residence in Washington, he lived in the third story hall bedroom at 502 Pennsylvania Avenue, which he himself described as "a miserable place." If it seemed miserable to Walt, who was rather more than callous to the nature of his surroundings, it must certainly have appeared squalid to others.

There were times when Walt thought of leaving Washington. Once he had some temptation to transfer his hospital activities to Nashville. A friend who wrote him from there offered other attractions in addition to the opportunity of ministering to soldiers, but Walt stayed in Washington. At times he returned to his old hope of lecturing, but there was little to encourage his ambition. From Brooklyn on November 17, 1863, he wrote to his friend, Charles W. Eldridge:

I feel to devote myself more and more to the work of my life, which is making poems. I must bring out *Drum Taps*. I *must* be continually bringing out poems—now is the hey day—I shall range along the high plateau of my life and capacity for a few years now, & then swiftly descend.

Soon after his return to Washington, his brother Andrew, who had long been sick, died. Walt had expected this event, but it increased his loneliness. He was not, however, without warm friendships in Washington. His affection for O'Connor continued for many years, though it ultimately broke. Walt never could be as enthusiastic a denouncer of slavery as O'Connor was and demanded that his friends should be.

Mrs. O'Connor, Walt remembered as "a superb woman without shams or brags—just a woman." He said of her, "She does not write; that gives her more time to get at the essentials of life." She made her home scarcely less than a social and literary center for aspiring and restless young men. Eldridge was often there and so was Edmund Clarence Stedman, then a war correspondent and poet, but later a banker and man of letters. Thither also came John Burroughs. He and Walt first encountered each other during a ramble in the woods on a Sunday afternoon and they became warm admirers of each other. Walt often breakfasted at the Burroughs' home on Sunday morning; never once did he arrive on time but Mrs. Burroughs forgave him. People were in the habit of forgiving Walt, and he was in the habit of giving them abundant 'occasion to exercise forgiveness toward him. He was extremely careless of his social obligations.[1]

One other of Walt's friendships should be mentioned. Peter Doyle was a big young Irishman who had served as a Confederate soldier, had been captured and paroled. He was only eighteen at the close of the war in 1865, and he earned two dollars a day as driver of a horse-car in Washington. He was illiterate, and his friendship for Whitman never kindled in him any literary ambitions. After the war, and for many years, he served as baggage master on the Colonial and Federal Express between Washington and Boston. He came to be Walt Whitman's most intimate friend. Whitman's letters to him are well known under the title *Calamus*. That, too, became the title of a group of Whitman's poems. Much has been written about this friendship and it need not be repeated here.[2]

Walt's first breakdown in the summer of 1864

began with dizziness and faintness and developed into a general breakdown, sending him back to Brooklyn for the remainder of the summer and the early autumn. The doctors called it malaria and a result of the bad air in the hospitals. As cold weather came on he returned to Washington. His letters from Brooklyn were full of his hope for the publication of *Drum-Taps*. In one of his letters he said, "I intend to move heaven and earth to publish my *Drum-Taps* as soon as I am able to go around."

While Walt continued his visits to the hospitals and continued to receive and expend money for use in such visits, his mind was increasingly on his unpublished manuscript of *Drum-Taps* and his hope of a new edition of *Leaves of Grass*.

He never succeeded in securing a publisher for *Drum-Taps*. When at length it appeared, it was published at his own expense. Fortunately for him at that time he had an income and was able to provide the money for the printing of it. Of these two books he wrote on January 6, 1865, to O'Connor from Brooklyn:

Drum-Taps has none of the perturbations of *Leaves of Grass*. I am satisfied with *Leaves of Grass* (by far the most of it) as expressing what was intended, namely, to express by sharp-cut self-assertion, One's-Self, and also, or may be, still more, to map out, to throw together for American use, a gigantic embryo or skeleton of Personality, fit for the West, for native models; but there are a few things I shall carefully eliminate in the next issue and a few more I shall considerably change.

I see I have said I consider *Drum-Taps* superior to *Leaves of Grass*. I probably mean as a piece of art and from the more simple winning nature of the subject and also because I have in it only succeeded to my satisfaction in removing all superfluity—verbal superfluity, I mean. I delight to make a poem where I feel clear that not a word but is an indispensable part thereof and my meaning.

Still *Leaves of Grass* is dear to me, always dearest to me as my first-born, as daughter of my life's first hopes, doubts, and the putting in form of those days efforts and aspirations. True, I see now some things in it I should not put in if I were to write now, but yet I shall certainly let them stand, even if but for proofs of phases passed away. . . .

In reading the foregoing letter, one can not fail to be interested in Walt's expressions "I see I have said" and "I probably mean." Walt was not always sure what he had said or precisely what he had meant by it. There was a vagueness in his own mind, a lack of sharp focus of intellectual definition.

In February, 1865, Walt secured what he so long had hoped for, an appointment to a clerkship. Through the constant pressure of his friends, he obtained a desk in the Indian Bureau in the Department of the Interior. He certainly was not appointed because of any need for his services. The Department of the Interior, and probably every other department of the Government, was overrun with clerks whose appointment was secured through political favor, or because of their real or imaginary services on the battle-field or in political life. A house-cleaning had to come in time. But the Republican party had been returned to power. There was no danger that superfluous clerkships would bring about any sudden reformation. An extra clerk or two did not greatly matter.

Walt was very happy. Writing to J. T. Trowbridge, on March third, he told him that he was working in the Indian office a few hours a day and that he had a sufficiently remunerative desk. His friends saw to it that it became more remunerative. He had two swift promotions and soon was receiving sixteen hundred dollars a year, the largest sum he had ever received, and he had very little to do for the government. He returned to the hospitals "moving around regularly but not to excess," as he described it. He told Trowbridge that he spent "a couple of hours a day or evenings in the hospitals." As nearly as we can learn from his diary, his hospital visits in 1865 were mainly on Sunday afternoons.

In fairly good health, but with some lack of his former vigor, Walt remained in Washington until after the second inauguration of President Lincoln. His description of this event we shall have occasion later to refer to. A few days later Walt secured whatever leave of absence was

necessary and returned to Brooklyn without any
loss of pay and without any serious interruption
of his work. Again he made ineffectual effort to
procure a publisher for *Drum-Taps*. While he
was at home with his mother in Brooklyn, the
shocking news came to him, as it came to the whole
country, that Abraham Lincoln had been mur-
dered.

VI

WALT WHITMAN saw Abraham Lincoln as he said in one of his letters, perhaps twenty or thirty times. Twice they were in the same room, but they never spoke to each other. Walt, in writing to his mother, told her that he and the President exchanged nods as he happened to see the President on his way to or from the soldiers' home where Lincoln lived in the summer-time. Those nods, however, were not evidences of recognition. It is doubtful if they were given to Walt as an individual. Lincoln, as he rode on horseback, was usually preoccupied and returned the salutations of people on the sidewalks without noticing particularly who they were or how many there were of them. Walt told his own story of the second inaugural and of the reception that evening. Although his memoranda of the war which he advertised as having been written on the spot were all edited afterward, these two paragraphs appear to be essentially as Walt wrote them at the time. This is his description of the President's ride to the Capitol on the morning of March 4, 1865.

The President very quietly rode down to the Capitol
in his own carriage, by himself, on a sharp trot, about
noon, either because he wished to be on hand to sign
bills, etc., or to get rid of marching in line with the
absurd procession, the muslin Temple of Liberty and the
Pasteboard Monitor. I saw him on his return at three
o'clock, after the performance was over. He was in his
plain two-horse barouche, and look'd very much worn
and tired; the lines, indeed, of vast responsibilities, upon
his dark brown face; yet all the old goodness, tenderness,
sadness and canny shrewdness, underneath the furrows.
(I have never seen the man without feeling that he is one
to become personally attach'd to; for his combination of
purest, heartiest tenderness, and native Western ever
rudest forms of manliness.) By his side sat his little boy,
of ten years. There were no soldiers, only a lot of
civilians, with huge yellow scarfs over their shoulders,
riding around the carriage. (At the Inaugural four
years ago, he rode down and back again, surrounded by a
dense mass of arm'd cavalry men, eight deep, with drawn
sabres; and there were sharp-shooters station'd at every
corner on the route.)[1]

Walt did not witness the first inaugural but
heard it described by witnesses and his judgment
of the contrast between the two occasions was
essentially correct. Walt attended the formal reception at the White House following the inauguration. He got inside but he certainly did not
succeed into getting in the line of those who shook
hands with the President or he would not have
failed to mention it. This is his account of the
reception.

I ought to make mention of the closing Levee of Saturday night last. Never was such a compact jam in front of the White House—all the grounds fill'd, and away out to the spacious side-walks. I was there, as I took a notion to go—was in the rush inside with the crowd—surg'd along the passageways, the Blue and other rooms, and through the great East room (upholster'd like a stage parlor). Crowds of country people, some very funny. Fine music from the Marine band, off in a side place. . . . I saw Mr. Lincoln, drest all in black, with white kid gloves, and a claw-hammer coat, receiving, as in duty bound, shaking hands, looking very disconsolate, and as if he would give anything to be somewhere else.[2]

This was the second time that President Lincoln and Walt Whitman were in the same room at the same time. The other was on Monday, October 31, 1864. Walt went to the White House to see John Hay and to secure if possible a pass to New York and return. John Hay procured the pass in order that Walt might go home and vote and if possible induce some of his friends to vote for Lincoln. In his diary for that day Walt told all there was to tell about that visit.

Called at the President's house on John Hay. Saw Mr. Lincoln standing, talking with a gentleman, apparently a dear friend.[3]

The interesting thing about this record is that Lincoln and Whitman were near enough together so that if Lincoln had any interest in Whitman, or if Whitman had felt justified in asking any favors of Lincoln, they would certainly have met. John Hay, who was always favorably disposed toward Walt, did not say "Just wait a minute, Mr. Whitman, till the President is at liberty, and I will introduce you. He has read your poetry and has seen you pass and I know he would like to shake your hand." John Hay said nothing of the kind. Walt Whitman did not ask to be introduced nor did he even feel at liberty to inquire the name of the man who was talking with Lincoln. He probably was nearer to Lincoln at that moment than ever before or afterward; neither then nor at any other time, did they meet.

It ought to be noted, however, that Whitman felt his heart going out to Lincoln from that moment as it had never done before. Simply being where he could see the great President, face to face with a friend, and unconsciously revealing his character in human relations, deeply impressed Walt Whitman.

In 1885 Allen Thorndike Rice, Editor of the *North American Review*, conceived the idea of preparing a volume of reminiscences of men who had actually known Lincoln.[4] He believed, and was correct in believing, that such a book would be a permanent storehouse of material for biographers and historians and would have wide popular interest. James Redpath, organizer and for many years manager of the famous Lecture Bureau that bore his name, called on Walt Whitman then living at Camden, to invite him to prepare one of these papers. He outlined the plan of Rice as follows:

He has conceived the plan of procuring a collection of papers, that united in one volume, will be a permanent memorial to Lincoln. He has set about to procure the reminiscences of all the eminent Americans who came into personal relations with him—each man to tell his story, whether it shall be short or long.

In a subsequent letter to Walt, Redpath enlarged slightly upon Rice's plan. He said:

Mr. Rice has got the ambition of editing a work which can never be superseded. He proposes to get every man of note now living who ever met Lincoln to write down in plain words and as accurately as the human memory will record, just how Lincoln looked, just what impression Lincoln made on him.

Walt Whitman was under no temptations to omit anything that he knew about Lincoln. He was paid at the rate of twenty dollars a thousand words and he used as many words as he could easily do. The story he told of hearing Lincoln address a regiment from the balcony of the National Hotel, is correct. It was not an Illinois Regiment but the One Hundred and Fortieth Indiana. The speech itself apparently did not make much impression upon Walt. It was, however, a speech of some importance. The date was March 17, 1865. Jefferson Davis and Robert E. Lee had long been in favor of enlisting negroes in the Confederate

Army and offering freedom as a reward to each slave who so enlisted and fought. This proposal stirred Lincoln to indignation and he said that while he would not like to see any man enslaved, if there were any one who deserved to be a slave it was he who would fight to hold his own race in slavery and accept his personal freedom as a reward. Walt's recollection of that day, however, was of the appearance of Lincoln, and he maintained that a photograph of Lincoln made on that occasion was the best that could anywhere be found.

Walt Whitman saw Lincoln as he passed through New York on his way toward his inauguration in Feburary, 1861, and Walt saw him in Washington about as many times as he estimated in his article. Virtually all he had to tell about Lincoln he included in his article for the *North American Review* volume. We are the more sure of this because, when Walt had occasion to use this material again, as he did three years later, he had nothing to add to it. On June 16, 1888, Horace Traubel recorded concerning Walt:

Asked Mrs. Davis to bring up the *N. A. Review* Lincoln book . . . he will use his own essay on Lincoln in that volume in November Boughs. Wished to know if the printers could work from the book? And would the N. A. R. people object to his including this in the book?

Whitman read very little of what other people wrote. His literary friends in Washington were not able to remember that they ever saw him with a book in his hand or a newspaper in his pocket. But when he was preparing his material for *November Boughs,* it occurred to him that it would be well to read what the other contributors to the *North American Review* volume had said about Lincoln. On June 30, 1888, Traubel records:

W. Reading the *N. A. Review* Lincoln volume when I entered. Closed it, took off his spectacles and said: "Lincoln don't need adorers, .worshippers—he needs friends. I take this book up a little now and then to see what can be made of it. The great danger with Lincoln for the next fifty years will be that he will be overdone, overexplained—made a good deal too much of—gather about himself a rather mythical aureole."

Nothing that Walt read or remembered suggested anything new of importance that he could tell about Abraham Lincoln. This is his essay as it originally appeared in the *North American Review* Volume and was reprinted practically without alteration in *November Boughs:*

PERSONAL REMINISCENCES OF
ABRAHAM LINCOLN

BY WALT WHITMAN

Glad am I to give even the most brief and shorn testimony in memory of Abraham Lincoln. Everything I heard about him authentically, and every time I saw him (and it was my fortune through 1862 to '65 to see, or pass a word with, or watch him, personally, perhaps

twenty or thirty times), added to and annealed my respect and love at the passing moment. And as I dwell
on what I myself heard or saw of the mighty Westerner,
and blend it with the history and literature of my age,
and of what I can get of all ages, and conclude it with
his death, it seems like some tragic play, superior to all
else I know—vaster and fierier and more convulsionary,
for this America of ours, than Eschylus or Shakespeare
ever drew for Athens or for England. And then the
Moral permeating, underlying all! the Lesson that none
so remote, none so illiterate—no age, no class—but may
directly or indirectly read!

From my Note-book in 1864, at Washington City, I
find this memorandum, under date of August 12:

I see the President almost every day, as I happen to
live where he passes to or from his lodgings out of town.
He never sleeps at the White House during the hot
season, but has quarters at a healthy location, some three
miles north of the city, the Soldiers' Home, a United
States military establishment. I saw him this morning
about 8:30 coming in to business, riding on Vermont
Avenue, near L Street. He always has a company of
twenty-five or thirty cavalry, with sabres drawn, and
held upright over their shoulders. The party makes no
great show in uniforms or horses. Mr. Lincoln, on the
saddle, generally rides a good-sized, easy-going gray
horse, is dress'd in plain black, somewhat rusty and
dusty; wears a black stiff hat, and looks about as
ordinary in attire, &c., as the commonest man. A
lieutenant, with yellow straps, rides at his left, and following behind, two by two, come the cavalry men in their
yellow-striped jackets. They are generally going at a
slow trot, as that is the pace set them by the One they
wait upon. The sabres and accoutrements clank, and
the entirely unornamental *cortege* as it trots toward

Lafayette Square arouses no sensation, only some curious stranger stops and gazes. I see very plainly ABRAHAM LINCOLN's dark brown face, with the deep cut lines, the eyes, &c., always to me with a latent sadness in the expression. We have got so that we always exchange bows, and very cordial ones.

Sometimes the President goes and comes in an open barouche. The cavalry always accompany him, with drawn sabres. Often I notice as he goes out evenings— and sometimes in the morning, when he returns early—he turns off and halts at the large and handsome residence of the Secretary of War on K Street, and holds conference there. If in his barouche, I can see from my window he does not alight, but sits in the vehicle, and Mr. Stanton comes out to attend him. Sometimes one of his sons, a boy of ten or twelve, accompanies him, riding at his right on a pony.

Earlier in the summer I occasionally saw the President and his wife, toward the latter part of the afternoon, out in a barouche, on a pleasure ride through the city. Mrs. Lincoln was dressed in complete black, with a long crape veil. The equipage is of the plainest kind, only two horses, and they nothing extra. They pass'd me once very close, and I saw the President in the face fully, as they were moving slow, and his look, though abstracted, happen'd to be directed steadily in my eye. He bow'd and smiled, but far beneath his smile I noticed well the expression I have alluded to. None of the artists or pictures have caught the subtle and indirect expression of this man's face. One of the great portrait painters of two or three centuries ago is needed.

Abraham Lincoln's was really one of those characters, the best of which is the result of long trains of cause and effect—needing a certain spaciousness of time, and perhaps even remoteness, to properly enclose them—having unequaled influence on the shaping of this Republic (and therefore the world) as to-day, and then far more important in the future. Thus the time has by no means yet come for a thorough measurement of him. Nevertheless, we who live in his era—who have seen him, and heard him, face to face, and are in the midst of, or just parting from, the strong and strange events which he and we have had to do with, can in some respects bear valuable, perhaps indispensable testimony concerning him.

I should first like to give what I call a very fair and characteristic likeness of Lincoln, as I saw him and watched him one afternoon in Washington, for nearly half an hour, not long before his death. It was as he stood on the balcony of the National Hotel, Pennsylvania Avenue, making a short speech[5] to the crowd in front, on the occasion either of a set of new colors presented to a famous Illinois regiment, or of the daring capture, by the Western men, of some flags from "the enemy," (which latter phrase, by the by, was not used by him at all in his remarks.) How the picture happened to be made I do not know, but I bought it a few days afterward in Washington, and it was endorsed by every one to whom I showed it. Though hundreds of portraits have been made, by painters and photographers (many to pass on, by copies, to future times), I have never seen one yet that in my opinion deserved to be called a perfectly *good likeness;* nor do I believe there is really such a one in existence. May I not say too, that, as there is no entirely competent and emblematic likeness of Abraham Lincoln in picture or statue, there is not—perhaps cannot be—any fully appropriate literary statement or summing-up of him, yet in existence.

The best way to estimate the value of Lincoln is to think what the condition of America would be today, if he had never lived—never been President. His nomina-

tion and first election were mainly accidents, experiments.
Severely viewed, one cannot think very much of American
Political Parties, from the beginning, after the Revolutionary War, down to the present time. Doubtless, while
they have had their uses—have been and are "the grass on
which the cow feeds"—and indispensable economies of
growth—it is undeniable that under flippant names they
have merely identified temporary passions, or freaks, or
sometimes prejudice, or hatred. The only thing like a
great and worthy idea vitalizing a party and making it
heroic was the enthusiasm in '64 for re-electing Abraham
Lincoln, and the reason behind that enthusiasm.

How does this man compare with the acknowledged
"Father of his country?" Washington was modeled on
the best Saxon, and Franklin of the age of the Stuarts
(rooted in the Elizabethan period)—was essentially a
noble Englishman, and just the kind needed for the
occasions and the times of 1776-'83. Lincoln, underneath his practicality, was far less European, far more
Western, original, essentially non-conventional, and had
a certain sort of out-door or prairie stamp. One of the
best of the late commentators on Shakespeare (Professor
Dowden), makes the height and aggregate of his quality
as a poet to be, that he thoroughly blended the ideal with
the practical or realistic. If this be so, I should say that
what Shakespeare did in poetic expression, Abraham
Lincoln essentially did in his personal and official life. I
should say the invisible foundations and vertebra of his
character, more than any man's in history, were mystical,
abstract, moral and spiritual—while upon all of them
was built, and out of all of them radiated, under the
control of the average of circumstances, what the vulgar
call *horse-sense*, and a life often bent by temporary but
most urgent materialistic and political reasons.

He seems to have been a man of indomitable firmness

(even obstinacy) on rare occasions, involving great points; but he was generally very easy, flexible, tolerant, respecting minor matters. I note that even those reports and anecdotes intended to level him down, all leave the tinge of a favorable impression of him. As to his religious nature, it seems to me to have certainly been of the amplest, deepest-rooted kind.

But I do not care to dwell on the features presented so many times, and that will readily occur to every one in recalling Abraham Lincoln and his era. It is more from the wish—and it no doubt actuates others—to bring for our own sake, some record, however incompetent— some leaf or little wreath to place, as on a grave.

Already a new generation begins to tread the stage, since the persons and events of the Secession War. I have more than once fancied to myself the time when the present century has closed and a new one opened, and the men and deeds of that contest have become vague and mythical—fancied perhaps in some great Western city, or group collected together, or public festival, where the days of old, of 1863 and '4 and '5 are discussed—some ancient soldier sitting in the background as the talk goes on, and betraying himself by his emotion and moist eyes— —like the journeying Ithacan at the banquet of King Alcinous, when the bard sings the contending warriors, and their battles on the plains of Troy:

"So from the sluices of Ulysses' eyes,
    Fast fell the tears, and sighs succeeded sighs."

I have fancied, I say, some such venerable relic of this time of ours, preserved to the next or still the next generation of America. I have fancied on such occasion, the young men gathering around; the awe, the eager questions. "What! have you seen Abraham Lincoln—

and heard him speak—and touched his hand? Have you, with your own eyes, looked on Grant, and Lee and Sherman?"

Dear to Democracy, to the very last! And among the paradoxes generated by America not the least curious, was that spectacle of all the kings and queens and emperors of the earth, many from remote distances, sending tributes of condolence and sorrow in memory of one raised through the commonest average of life—a rail-splitter and flat-boatman!

Considered from contemporary points of view—who knows what the future may decide?—and from the points of view of current Democracy and The Union (the only thing like passion or infatuation in the man was the passion for the Union of These States), Abraham Lincoln seems to me the grandest figure yet, on all the crowded canvas of the Nineteenth Century.

WALT WHITMAN.

VII

WHAT LINCOLN KNEW ABOUT WHITMAN

SOME years ago, Thomas Bird Mosher, preparing for the press one of his charming editions of Walt Whitman's writings, said in the preface that we have no knowledge that Lincoln ever read any of Whitman's poems. In his reprint of the first edition of *Leaves of Grass,* 1919, he said, "Until three years ago, no one actually knew that Lincoln had ever read *Leaves of Grass."* He then proceeded to set forth proof of what he called "the extraordinary statement" that Lincoln read this book "about 1857." The verification is found in *Personal Recollections of Abraham Lincoln,* by Henry B. Rankin.[1] The quotation is of marked interest:

When Walt Whitman's *Leaves of Grass* was first published, it was placed on the office table by Herndon. It had been read by several of us, and, one day, discussions hot and extreme had sprung up between office students and Mr. Herndon concerning its poetic merit, in which Dr. Bateman engaged with us, having entered, from his adjoining office. Later, quite a surprise occurred when we found that the Whitman poetry and our discussions had been engaging Lincoln's silent attention. After the rest of us had finished our criticism of some peculiar verses and of Whitman in general, as well as of each other's taste in literary matters and morals in particular, and had resumed our usual duties or had departed, Lincoln, who during the criticisms had been apparently in the unapproachable depths of one of his glum moods of meditative silence,—referred to elsewhere,—took up *Leaves of Grass* for his first reading of it. After half an hour or more of devotion to it, he turned back to the first pages and, to our general surprise, began to read aloud. . . . His rendering revealed a charm of new life in Whitman's versification. Save for a few comments on some broad allusions that Lincoln suggested could have been veiled, or left out, he commended the new poet's verses for their virility, freshness, unconventional sentiments, and unique forms of expression, and claimed that Whitman gave promise of a new school of poetry.

At his request, the book was left by Herndon on the office table. Time and again, when Lincoln came in, or was leaving, he would pick it up, as if to glance at it for only a moment, but instead he would often settle down in a chair and never stop without reading aloud such verses or pages as he fancied. His estimate of the poetry differed from any brought out in the office discussions. He foretold correctly the place the future would assign to Whitman's poems, and that *Leaves of Grass* would be followed by other and greater work. A few years later, immediately following the tragedy of Lincoln's assassination, Whitman wrote that immortal elegy, "O Captain! My Captain!" which became the nation's, aye, the world's funeral dirge for our First American. When I first read this requiem, its thrilling lines revived in my memory that quiet afternoon in the Springfield law-office, and Lincoln's first reading and comments on *Leaves of Grass*. That scene was so vividly recalled then as to become more firmly fixed in my memory than any other of the incidents at the Lincoln and Herndon office, and this is my apology for giving space for rehearsing it so fully here.

It is unfortunate, if this story came so vividly to Mr. Rankin's recollection in 1865, that he waited more than half a century before telling it. Dr. Newton Bateman was dead, William H. Herndon was dead. None of the other law students in their office was living. No one was left in 1916 to check up on the recollection of a very old man of an incident alleged to have occurred when he was a lad. It is astonishing, if Lincoln displayed this interest in Whitman, that Herndon, who was keeping account of his sayings and doings, his habits of dress and manner of walking and his way of eating an apple, and his almost total neglect of books, should not have mentioned that, along with Byron and Burns and Shakespeare, Lincoln admired Walt Whitman. Herndon owned a copy of *Leaves of Grass* but never mentioned Lincoln as reading it. At the time Herndon procured his copy of *Leaves of Grass,* about 1857, Lincoln was approaching his debate with Douglas, and was consequently in process of emerging as a noted figure in national politics. Herndon was watching him with Boswellian interest, taking notes on his sayings and doings, and preserving his memorabilia for subsequent use. Herndon, who was rhetorical

and poetical in his own mind and style, was careful
to make notes on Lincoln's literary tastes or the
lack of them.   It is remarkable that we should
have had to wait till long after Herndon was dead
to discover that *Leaves of Grass,* which Herndon
had bought, found a lover and defender in Lincoln.

Henry B. Rankin was born in Menard County,
Illinois, a county that passed very few votes for
Lincoln in 1860. Just why he should have studied
law in the intensely Republican office of Lincoln
and Herndon has never been explained. So far as
is known, he never claimed to have been a student
in the Lincoln and Herndon office until most of the
men were dead who could have contradicted him.
When he put forth the claim, at first with a discreet
vagueness as to the precise time which this apprenticeship covered, most of the men who could
have contradicted him kept silent in public. What
they said in private need not here be repeated.
They remembered, however, that Lincoln and
Herndon took in very few law students. They
could recall only two and these for no very great
length of time, and neither of them was named
Rankin. Lincoln advised young men to read law
at home as he had done, and pleaded that his almost
constant absence on the circuit and in his political
campaigning, made it impossible for him to super-
vise the studies of law students. The only compen-
sation which lawyers received from students working in their offices was the preparation or copying

of legal documents. The files of all the counties in which Lincoln practised have been searched for every scrap of paper bearing on any of Lincoln's known cases. Thus far, no document has been found in the handwriting of Mr. Rankin. The only time when Lincoln's office adjoined that of Newton Bateman was in the busy period after Lincoln had been nominated for the Presidency. He was permitted courteously to share the Governor's office, and receive his visitors there.

The only thing to be said about Mr. Rankin's recollection of Lincoln as a reader of *Leaves of Grass,* is that Mr. Rankin, in common with many other old men, mixed his memories with his imagination.

VIII

"HE LOOKS LIKE A MAN"

WE HAVE already recorded the fact that Walt Whitman was able to secure a desk in the Indian Bureau of the Department of the Interior. We shall presently have occasion to learn that he did not hold that position permanently, but was removed by Secretary James Harlan. The circumstances of his removal and the flood of literature which resulted will receive attention in a future chapter. The matter is referred to here because, while we are considering what Abraham Lincoln knew about Walt Whitman, we must take into account an alleged utterance of Lincoln relating to the poet.

After the death of Lincoln, his apotheosis began immediately. People who had met him, and others who had not, began to relate their memories of Lincoln, and to him were attributed innumerable utterances, some of them genuine and others more than doubtful.

> Lives of great men all remind us,
> That when we are safely dead,
> People will attribute to us,
> Many things we never said.

Lincoln's was and is a name to conjure with; and few men felt more sure of having scored in an argument than those who were able to quote from Lincoln some utterance that appeared to sustain their contention. Few alleged utterances of Lincoln have been more effectively used than one employed by William Douglas O'Connor in the beginning of his pamphlet, *The Good Gray Poet.*[1] Immediately after the introductory paragraphs, he related the incident which evoked the alleged quotation:

I treasure to my latest hour, with swelling heart and springing tears, the remembrance that Abraham Lincoln, seeing him for the first time from the window of the East Room of the White House as he passed slowly by, and gazing at him long with that deep eye which read men, said, in the quiet, sweet tone which those who have spoken with him will remember, and with a significant emphasis which the type can hardly convey—"Well, *he* looks like *a man!*" Sublime tribute, great words; but none too high for their object, the author of *Leaves of Grass*, Walt Whitman, of Brooklyn.

O'Connor's story that Lincoln seeing Whitman said, "Well, he looks like a man," rests on the testimony contained in a letter to Whitman from a person not known to him, and who professed to write from New York, July 30, 1865, and who signed himself "A. Van Rensellaer." The information in this letter, Whitman promptly conveyed to his hot-headed friend, William Douglas

O'Connor, who made effective use of it in his brochure, *The Good Gray Poet.*

Whitman afterward mislaid the letter, and it would appear that his closest friends were a trifle skeptical about the authenticity of the incident. Whitman was greatly pleased when the letter turned up. Horace Traubel tells the story under date of Sunday, November 25, 1888.[2]

W. was rather cranky tonight. Jumped on me for not having some message from Ferguson. "What the hell?" he asked two or three times. I got tired of hearing it, and asked him, "What the hell?" too. That made him laugh. I said: "If I'm doing so miserable bad, why don't you bounce me?" He looked indignant. for a minute, then said, "I couldn't: you wouldn't be bounced." "Then you'd better accept me the way I am." I was a bit mad myself. We don't have many tiffs. Finally he said: "Don't let's go on in that vein; I've something pleasanter here: what do you think of it?" He reached smilingly to the table, picked up a letter and handed it to me. I read the letter. "Is it for me?" I asked. It hardly seemed possible. "Yes, it's for your safe box: but you haven't said what you think of it." "What can I say? Only that I never expected to see the letter: you know you said a bit ago that you didn't think it would ever turn up again." He: "Well, it did turn up. Read it to me." I said: "I bet you know it by heart." "So I do: but I can listen to it again coming from your voice." I read:[3]

"New York, July 30, 1865.
"Dear Sir,
"Looking over a file of papers in the reading room, I saw a paragraph about your dismissal from the Interior

Department, and as I once read your book, I am moved to express my feelings in the matter. The act strikes me as pretty mean, but quite of a piece with Harlan's character. As I see you are in the Atty. Gen'l's office, I will call on you when I come to W. in a few days and tell you *in confidence* a little transaction I once had with Harlan a long time ago, which will show you the kind of a chap he is. I read your book when it first came out and though I admit a good deal of it was blind to me, I saw considerable that struck me as first class, though I don't pretend to much judgment in such matters. Any how, I don't see anything worse in what Harlan makes so much of than what is in old Bill Shakespear and the Bible, and dashed in pretty thick too. Some folks are more squemish than me, though.

"Perhaps you might like to hear something Mr. Lincoln once said of you, which you probably never heard of. It wasn't much to say, but the way he said it struck me a good deal. It was in the winter time, I think in '64, I went up to the White House with a friend of mine, an M. C., who had some business with the President. He had gone out, so we didn't stop, but coming down-stairs, quite near the door we met the President coming in, and we stept back into the East Room and stood near the front windows where my friend had a confab with him. It didn't last more than three or four minutes, but there was something about a letter which my friend had handed the President and Mr. Lincoln had read it and was holding it in his hand and thinking it over, and looking out of the window when you went by, quite slow, with your hands in the breast pocket of your overcoat and a sizable hat on your head pretty well up, just as I have often seen you on Broadway. Mr. Lincoln, asked who you were or something like that. I spoke up and said, mentioning your name, that you had written *Leaves of Grass*, etc.

New York, July 30 1865

Dear Sir,

Looking over a pile of papers in the reading room I saw a paragraph about your dismissal from the Interior Department, and as I once read your book I am moved to express my feelings in the matter. The act strikes me as pretty mean but quite of a piece with Harlan's character. As I see you are in the Atty Genl's office I will call on you when I come to W. in a few days and tell you in confidence a little transaction I once had with Harlan, long time ago, which will show you the kind of chap he is. I read your book when it first came out and though I must admit a good deal of it was blind to me, I saw considerable which struck me as first class, though I dont pretend to much judgment in such matters. Anyhow I didn't see anything in

THE "VAN RENSELLAER" LETTER

what Harlan makes so much of than
what is in old Bill Shakspear and the
Bible; and dashed in every thing too.
Some folk are more squeamish than
me though. — Perhaps you might like
to hear something Mr Lincoln once said
of you, which you probably never heard
of. It wasnt much to say, but the way
he said it struck me a good deal
It was in the winter time, I think in
'64 I went up to the White House with
a friend of mine, an M.C., who had
some business with the President.
He had gone out, & we didnt stop, but
coming down stairs, quite near the door
we met the President coming in and
we stept back into the East Room
and stood near the front windows,
where my friend had a confab with
him. It didnt last more than three or
four minutes but there was something
about a letter which my friend had
handed the President, and Mr Lincoln
had read it and was holding it in his
hand like one thinking it over, and

looking out of the window when you
went by, quite slow, with your hands
in the breast pocket of your overcoat
and a sizeable felt hat on and your
head pretty well up, just as I have often
seen you on Broadway. Mr Lincoln
asked who you were, or something like
that. I spoke up and said mentioning
your name and that you had written
'Leaves of Grass,' etc, Mr Lincoln didn't
say anything but took a good long look
till you were quite gone by, then he
says— (I can't give you the way of
saying it, but it was quite emphatic and
odd) "Well", he says, "He looks like a
man." He said it pretty loud but
in a sort of absent way and with the
emphasis on the words I have underscored.
He didn't say anymore but begun to talk
again about the letter and in a minute or
so, we went off. Seeing your name
just now in the paper put me in mind
of it and I thought it was an item
you might like to know. It was the
only time I ever spoke to Mr Lincoln

though I see him often.

I expect to be in Washington on my way down South in a few days and will take the freedom of giving you a call. Please dont mention my name in connexion with what I write about Harlan.

I'll explain why when I see you and you will see the reason for not spreading it round.

With respect &c,

truly yours
A Van Rensselaer

Mr. Lincoln didn't say anything but took a long look till you were quite gone by. Then he says—(I can't give you his way of saying it but it was quite emphatic and odd) 'Well,' he says, '*he* looks like a *man*.' He said it pretty loud but in a sort of absent way and with the emphasis on the words I have underscored. He didn't say any more but began to talk about the letter and in a minute or so we went off. Seeing your name just now in the paper put me in mind of it and I thought it was an item you might like to know. It was the only time I ever spoke to Mr. Lincoln though I saw him often.

"I expect to be in Washington on my way down South in a few days and will take the freedom of giving you a call. Please don't mention my *name* in connexion with what I write about Harlan. I'll explain why when I see you, and you will see the reason for not spreading it around.

"With respects, etc.
"Truly yours,
"A.   Van Rensellaer."

Traubel proceeded with his narrative:

W. must have seen the big smile on my face. He looked extra pleased himself. "I am twice glad to see the letter again: once glad for myself, once glad for you." I said: "I'm a hundred times glad myself." Then he said: "I think that letter will convince you: I have sometimes thought you had an idea we were romancing a bit in telling that story about Lincoln: now you can see for yourself that we've kept literally prosaically to the figures—have added nothing to them." I turned the letter over and over in my hands. "This is the real thing," I said. "This puts the Lincoln story on ice." W. was heartily amused. "You are a damned impertinent snip after all: you wouldn't believe until you were convinced, as you say, you held off: you half thought I was lying—William, too—all the fellows. Well, the dispute is settled, now or have you still some suspicions? maybe you think the letter is forged." We laughed together. I kissed him good night. He held my hand for an extra clasp. "Don't let our fight prejudice you against me," he said.

The incident as related in the letter of "A. Van Rensellaer" is not inherently improbable. It might easily have occurred just as it is told. Nor is it at all to be supposed that Whitman invented the story in 1865 and forged the letter in 1888; his inquiry whether Traubel thought the letter a forgery is beside the mark.

The difficulty lies in the fact that so far as has thus far been shown, there is no information about this man Van Rensellaer, and we have good reason to believe he did not exist. The letter is vague, intentionally vague, in those particulars which might assist in making its authenticity certain.

There was an A. Van Rensselaer, living in New York at the time, and there was but one who was of suitable age to have been the author of this letter. He, as his relatives agree, could not have written it. He was a rich man, living a detached life, spending much of his time in foreign travel, and having no contacts out of which this experience could have come. Moreover, that is not the kind of letter he would have written. He was not a man who hung about public reading-rooms to use the daily papers; he had his own well-appointed library. He was not at all interested in politics or in Whitman, and such controversies as one which might arise over the discharge of a department clerk on the supposed charge of having written an improper book would have been among the last things to interest him. If he had written a letter, it would have been a dignified missive, on his own stamped stationery. This letter, without street address, with faulty grammar, and reference to "old Bill Shakespear" is not in character.[4]

But Dr. Alexander Van Rensselaer had an elder brother, Brigadier-General Henry Van Rensselaer, a graduate of West Point, a member of the staff of General Scott. He was in Washington often, and he might possibly have been aroused to interest in a matter that would not have concerned his brother. Could he have been the man? Might the "A. Van Rensellaer" have been "H. Van Rensselaer" with a hastily signed initial?

The original letter, I have carefully examined. There is no doubt about the initial; it is not "H" but "A."

The War Department had some additional information concerning Brigadier-General Henry Van Rensselaer, including letters and reports from him. He was accustomed to sign his name "H. Van Rennsselaer," but his "H" could not be mistaken for an "A." His double "s" w~ unmistakable, for he used the long, old fashioned f-like "s." There is one additional reason for believing that he did not write the Whitman letter July 30, 1865, which is that the War Department records show that he died March 23, 1864.

"But some Van Rensselaer must have written it! Surely, no one would have had any motive for inventing the story!"

On the contrary, the experience of any man who has ever had a controversy that got into the newspapers knows there are many people who crave vicarious publicity, and who take pen in hand to write to men whose names they see in print, offering wholly unreliable information. Court records show that such people often have got as far as the witness stand and have told wholly imaginary stories in important murder trials. They even write detailed confessions, not to give false clews, but to gain a sort of impersonal notoriety. But do such people write letters and withhold their names? They certainly do.

Let us examine this document for a moment. This letter written to Whitman in the summer of 1865 tells that the writer had called on Lincoln in the White House, *he thinks* in the winter of 1864. That was a very few months previous, and in the interval, Lincoln had died. Let me illustrate from my own experience. I had occasion to call at the White House just before the United States declared war on Germany. If I had been writing

about it in the following summer, would I have
said that I talked with Woodrow Wilson "*I think*
in the winter of 1917"? I have more than one way
of reminding myself that the date was January 31,
1917, the very day on which President Wilson received his communication that Germany intended
to resume unrestricted submarine warfare. Still
again, I had occasion to call at the White House
a few days before President Harding went out of
it for the last time. If shortly after his funeral I
had been telling about it, would I have said that
"*I think*" it was in the summer of 1923? In any
one of several ways I can fix the date as June
7, 1923. The man who in 1865 guessed uncertainly
that he had called on Lincoln "in the winter of
1864" had reason for his uncertainty. He was
vague about the matter because the whole story
was a lie.

The writer of this letter requested Whitman not
to disclose his name, saying that he soon would call
on Whitman and give him further information.
He never called. And he never wrote to explain
why he did not call.

But there is still one last and wholly convincing
reason. The original letter, which I have examined, shows that the writer started to sign one
name and changed to another which he misspelled.
He wrote "Van Rensellaer" exactly as a man
would be likely to write it who was not accustomed
to it, and exactly as no Van Rensselaer would ever

have written it. The Van Rensselaers hope in hell
his soul may dwell who singles the "s" and doubles
the "l."

Who did write it? We do not know. Some one
who wrote a round, Spencerian hand, and had a
limited education but a large imagination. Perhaps he was one of those men of good handwriting
who before the days of addressographs found
irregular employment in the "envelope dumps."
When he was out of employment, he could find
warmth and shelter in the public reading-room,
and was interested in seeing how easily and how
often he could "start something." Without such
men what would become of the "Vox Populi"
columns in the daily papers?

There is one other interesting possibility. Whitman had some friends who were loyal enough to
have written it, and not too good. O'Connor himself was one of them. Whitman himself did not
write it, and he really believed in it: but his friends
were fully justified in their skepticism.

But while Whitman did not himself forge this
letter, it is not easy to believe that he was deceived
by it. He read it many times and with care. As
he admitted to Traubel, he knew it by heart. We
can not be sure that his mislaying of it was wholly
accidental. O'Connor could have misspelled the
signature and Traubel would not have been likely
to detect the mistake, but it was not a letter that
would have been safe in the hands of discriminat-

ing people.   Careless in almost everything else,
Walt Whitman was a meticulous proof-reader, and
he knew how the old New York families spelled
their names.   It did not surprise him that his
associates had their doubts about the letter; he was
in position to know that their doubts were justified.

Whoever wrote it, the letter is a fraud.   Still,
Walt Whitman did look like a man, even though
Abraham Lincoln did not say it, or know how
Whitman looked.

IX

THE LAST DAYS OF LINCOLN

WE LEFT Abraham Lincoln in the White House on the first day of January, 1863, signing the final Proclamation of Emancipation, and steadying his arm that had become stiff and numb by reason of a long period of hand-shaking. He had need of all his steadiness of nerve and strength of purpose in the days that followed. Not yet did victory perch upon the banners of the nation. Not yet did the President find a general whose stubborn determination could match the brilliant strategy of Robert E. Lee. In the middle of that year came Lee's invasion of Pennsylvania that ended in the defeat of his superb army at Gettysburg. Simultaneously with that victory came the fall of Vicksburg, where General Grant again emerged into public notice, a short reticent man, with a stubby full beard, and the butt of a cigar between his teeth. A little later, Lincoln made him Commander-in-Chief of the Army of the United States, but still the war dragged on.[1]

Another New Year's came, with another siege

of hand-shaking, and more swollen knuckles and stiff muscles. Still the war did not end. It began to seem as though it would never end. Battles were more frequent and losses were more heavy and though the Union armies gained ground, it was at heavy cost.

In the summer of 1864, the political conventions were held. The Democrats nominated Major-General George B. McClellan. The Republican party, changing its name to the Union Party, nominated Abraham Lincoln. They were not very enthusiastic about it, but there was nothing else they could very well do. As Lincoln himself said, they thought it well not to swap horses while crossing a stream. During that summer and the greater part of the fall, it seemed that Lincoln would be defeated. However, Sherman's victories in Georgia, and Grant's slow progress in grinding Lee's army to pieces, turned the tide of popular favor. Lincoln was reelected. Walt Whitman, who was a rather luke-warm abolitionist and for a time no great admirer of Lincoln, not only voted for him but did some work toward his reelection.

General Grant, moving forward by slow inches, and losing men every inch, determined to "fight it out on that line if it took all summer." It took all summer, and all winter, too. From time to time it appeared that peace was at hand, but peace and victory were long deferred.

The burden on the President's shoulders grew

daily more heavy. Where to find the troops, how to fill the gaps in the ever-thinning ranks, how to keep the Cabinet working happily together, and Congress in a mood to further his plans, how to maintain discipline in the army, and still pardon the boys who were sentenced to be shot, all these responsibilities deepened the lines on Lincoln's face and deepened also the agony in his heart.

At last came the spring, and with it the fall of Petersburg and the evacuation of Richmond. Jefferson Davis fled south, and Lee's army retreated west with Grant in hot pursuit. At Five Forks General Sheridan defeated Lee in a cavalry action, and Lee's position became insupportable. On Palm Sunday, April 9, 1865, General Robert E. Lee surrendered the Army of Northern Virginia to General Ulysses S. Grant at Appomattox Court House.

The end of the war was at hand. The nation gave a jubilant shout. Abraham Lincoln's face lit up with a wan and thankful smile.

Then came the bullet of the assassin.

On Friday evening, April fourteenth, Abraham Lincoln was shot. He died early the next morning.

Walt Whitman was not in Washington when he died.

X

"THE GOOD GRAY POET"

ABRAHAM LINCOLN and Walt Whitman were
alike in this that they both attained to unusual
stature in early youth. They shot up suddenly,
Lincoln with so violent catapult toward the sky
that he absorbed in the process the energy that
should normally have been distributed over a number of succeeding years. But Lincoln retained till
death his dark brown, almost black, hair, while
Whitman was growing gray at thirty. At the close
of the war, Whitman was forty-six, and wholly
gray. He was not without a realizing sense of the
value to him of this feature of his appearance. He
cultivated his grayness, and accentuated it in his
attire. His long and picturesque hair and full
beard alone would have made him conspicuous, and
he was not of a mind not to know the full worth
of these characteristics. There came a time when
they served him particularly well, and an ardent
friend, with a gift for alliteration and a temperament that loved a fight, utilized the lack of pigment
in Walt's hair and the habitual color of his raiment,

and gave him another name than that to which he had been born. His admirers quickly adopted it, and Walt Whitman became "The Good Gray Poet." To be sure there were some who said of this sobriquet that it could not quite be contradicted as sweepingly as Voltaire denied the veracity of the title "The Holy Roman Empire," declaring that it was neither holy nor Roman nor an Empire. Walt Whitman was undeniably gray.

In order to bring together the instances in which Lincoln and Whitman were alleged to have seen each other, it was necessary to mention the circumstances that gave rise to the story that Lincoln had said of Whitman, "He looks like a man." It was necessary to state somewhat in advance of chronological order that Walt Whitman did not long retain his clerkship in the Indian Bureau. This is the proper place to relate the whole story of the way in which Walt lost his comfortable and lucrative position.

The director of the budget of the United States has recently published statistics showing how enormously the pay-roll of the United States was increased during the World War and what an herculean task it has been to weed out some of the superfluous clerks, and how necessary it was that this should be done. Billions of dollars, he affirms, have already been saved in this way since the Armistice.

A similar situation prevailed in 1865, but it had

one feature that was more embarrassing. Washington was filled with partly disabled men who had lost arms or legs in the army and were disqualified for manual labor. Besides these were innumerable widows and daughters of soldiers who needed more money than their slender pension provided. Congress passed a resolution recommending that, other things being equal, clerical positions in the departments of the Government, should be given to soldiers and to soldiers' widows. But already there were far too many of them on the pay-roll for the work that was to be done.

Walt Whitman's only possible opportunity to secure a clerkship in 1865 lay in an exaggeration of his services in the hospital. The Department of the Interior seemed a favorable place for a possible opening. The Secretary of the Interior, Honorable John P. Usher, was one of the cabinet officers not to be reappointed. Furthermore, Mr. Usher was a man who liked to please his friends. His assistant, Judge William T. Otto, knew Whitman and wanted to see him provided for. J. Hubley Ashton, then assistant in the office of the Attorney-General, was also a warm supporter of Walt. Early in January, 1865, Whitman applied to Judge Otto for a clerkship, enclosing recommendations from John T. Trowbridge and others, calling attention to Walt's services to soldiers in the hospital. He sent to Mr. Ashton copies of these letters, and Ashton's personal influence with Otto secured for the poet the coveted clerkship in the office of Indian affairs, a bureau of the Department of the Interior. The salary to begin with was twelve hundred dollars a year. The examination was a formality, though Walt could have passed one if it had been necessary. The appointment was made on January twenty-fourth, and Walt had then only to take the oath and enter upon his duties.

Those duties were not arduous. There was already an excess of clerks in the Indian office. Walt Whitman was not appointed because his help was needed, but because his friends wanted to secure a place for him. Walt took such work as was assigned to him, which was very little, and it did not at all prevent his leaving for Brooklyn on an extended stay if he cared to leave. On May 11, 1865, he was promoted to a second-class clerkship, dating from the first of that month, at a salary of sixteen hundred dollars. Again it was Otto who brought about this happy result. Walt was opulent with his large salary, and he had as nearly nothing to do as even a department clerk in that chaotic period could have desired. He brought to his desk his *Leaves of Grass* and his *Drum-Taps* and found ample time during office hours to devote to their revision. So delightful a situation could hardly endure in a world of change and tragedy. A new king arose who knew not Joseph, and when he came to know about Walt he did not like him.

What ensued is so important, and has been so often related in divers portions and sundry manners, it is well to learn the full facts. The man who discharged Walt Whitman from his comfortable desk was the new Secretary, the Honorable James Harlan.

James Harlan was about the age of Whitman; he was born in Clark County, Illinois, August 26, 1820. His parents removed to Indiana when he was a small child, and he worked his way through Asbury, now De Pauw, University, at Greencastle, and was graduated August 20, 1845. He was an ardent Methodist, and often spoke in religious meetings. In the controversy that followed Whitman's discharge it was popular to say that he had been a Methodist preacher. He was not a minister, but a lawyer and politician, though he served for two years as President of a Methodist school in Iowa City, which town became his home. A strong opponent of slavery, he was one of the founders of the Republican party in Iowa, and in 1854 was elected to the United States Senate and reelected in 1860. He was one of the men whom Lincoln consulted, sending to the Senate for him, when Lincoln arrived in Washington in 1861, desiring particularly Harlan's advice as to the popularity of Chase as Secretary of the Treasury among Iowa Republicans. He was frequently called into counsel with Lincoln, and Lincoln valued his judgment, which did not always accord with his own and was given with great frankness. In the main, however, the two men agreed, and Harlan was one of Lincoln's warmest admirers. It was years after Lincoln's death before Harlan could trust himself to refer to Lincoln in a public address.

On the occasion of the Second Inaugural, Senator Harlan was appointed to escort Mrs. Lincoln to and from the service; and the Harlan family was in the receiving line with the Lincolns at the Inaugural Ball. The relation between the two families was intimate. Captain Robert T. Lincoln became attached to Senator Harlan's daughter, Mary, whom he later married. When Lincoln made his last public address, from a balcony of the White House, on the evening of April 11, 1865, Harlan was in the White House, and was publicly introduced by Lincoln at the close of the latter's address as one who was to share with the President the responsibilities of government, and Harlan spoke briefly but effectively. Harlan was one of the official delegation to attend the Lincoln funeral, and became a member of the National Committee in charge of the Memorial.

Lincoln's first Secretary of the Interior, Caleb B. Smith, was appointed to a district judgeship in 1863, and was succeeded by John P. Usher of Indiana, who resigned March 8, 1865, probably at Lincoln's suggestion. The resignation was promptly accepted, and Lincoln immediately appointed Harlan in his stead. The appointment by

the President and the confirmation by the Senate
both occurred March ninth, the day after Usher's
resignation, although Usher's retirement was not to
take place until May fifteenth. For several months
the Iowa papers had discussed the probability that
Harlan would be in the Lincoln Cabinet in the
second term, and had expressed satisfaction. Early
in January Harlan's correspondence showed that
he was considering the probability that he would
be offered the Secretaryship of the Interior. The
appointment was, under all the conditions, a very
natural one. There was gossip, however, as to
sectarian influence, and this gossip Whitman was
later very glad to accept as truth.[1]

While it was hanging in suspense who should be appointed Secretary of the Interior, (to take the place of
Caleb Smith,) the choice was very close between Mr.
Harlan and Col. Jesse K. Dubois, of Illinois. The latter
had many friends. He was competent, he was honest, and
he was a man. Mr. Harlan, in the race, finally gain'd
the Methodist interest, and got himself to be consider'd
as identified with it: and his appointment was apparently
ask'd for by that powerful body. Bishop Simpson, of
Philadelphia, came on and spoke for the selection. The
President was much perplex'd. The reasons for appoint-
ing Col. Dubois were very strong, almost insuperable—
yet the argument for Mr. Harlan, under the adroit position he had plac'd himself, was heavy. Those who press'd
him adduc'd the magnitude of the Methodists as a body,
their loyalty, more general and genuine than any other
sect—that they represented the West, and had a right
to be heard—that all or nearly all the other great de-

nominations had their representatives in the heads of the
government—that they as a body and the great sectarian
power of the West, formally ask'd Mr. Harlan's appointment—that he was of them, having been a Methodist
minister—that it would not do to offend them, but was
highly necessary to propitiate them.

Mr. Lincoln thought deeply over the whole matter.
He was in more than usual tribulation on the subject.
Let it be enough to say that though Mr. Harlan finally
receiv'd the Secretaryship, Col. Dubois came as near
being appointed as a man could, and not be. The decision was finally made one night about ten o'clock.
Bishop Simpson and other clergymen and leading persons
in Mr. Harlan's behalf had been talking long and
vehemently with the President. A member of Congress
who was pressing Col. Dubois' claims, was in waiting. The
President had told the Bishop that he would make a
decision that evening and that he thought it unnecessary
to be press'd any more on the subject. That night he
call'd in the M. C. above alluded to, and said to him: "Tell
Uncle Jesse that I want to give him this appointment,
and yet I can not. . . . I will do almost anything in
the world for him if I am able. I have thought the matter
all over, and under the circumstances think the
Methodists too good and too great a body to be slighted.
They have stood by the government, and help'd us their
very best. I have had no better friends, and as the case
stands, I have decided to appoint Mr. Harlan."

It was of course impossible for Whitman to have
known all this, and the story as he told it is not
complimentary to Lincoln. Harlan's correspondence has been published, and it shows no keen desire
on his part for a Cabinet position; he was com-

fortably located in the Senate, with a reasonable prospect of continued service there. His political future was safer if he stayed where he was, and he knew it and said so at the time. But he was entirely willing to accept a Cabinet position, if Lincoln desired him to do so and his Iowa constituents counted their State honored by his appointment, and it may be that among the many who supported the proposal for his appointment, were some prominent Methodists. It is true, also, that Jesse K. Dubois had many friends who desired to see him in the Cabinet: but there is no good reason to think that Lincoln was in any uncertainty as to whom he wanted and intended to appoint.

In whatever way the appointment was secured, it is evident that Harlan, or some man with equal courage, was needed in the Department. He was not able to keep it very long. The Cabinet suffered shipwreck in the stormy seas of Andrew Johnson's administration, and Harlan resigned July 27, 1866. Had Lincoln lived, there is no reason to doubt that Harlan would have served his full term with credit. As it was, he would now hardly be remembered as having been a member of the Cabinet had it not been that he discharged Walt Whitman from his clerkship. The letter dismissing him reads:

Department of the Interior,
        Washington, D. C., June 30th, 1865.
The services of Walter Whitman, of New York, as a

clerk in the Indian Office, will be dispensed with from
and after this date.

Jas. Harlan,
Secretary of the Interior.

Judge Otto inquired of Secretary Harlan the
reason for Walt's dismissal, and while Harlan declared that he never gave any reason excepting that
Walt was not needed in the Department, Otto
secured from Harlan enough of an admission to
seem to warrant the belief that Harlan had found a
copy of *Leaves of Grass* in Walt's desk and
thought it an indecent book.[2] He passed this information on to J. Hubley Ashton. Ashton
immediately secured for Walt a clerkship in the
Treasury Department. In effect, Walt had
simply been transferred from one desk where he
did little work for the Government to another
where he had equally large liberty. Very few people knew about it, and those who knew were mainly
satisfied that Walt still was provided with a comfortable living. But this did not satisfy William
Douglas O'Connor. Walt had been discharged by
a Methodist, a lawyer to be sure, but it was easy to
say that he had once been a Methodist preacher, a
statement which was not true but helped to make
it seem that he was probably a bigot. O'Connor
took nine weeks to brood over this matter, and then
brought out a pamphlet, one of the most brilliant
pieces of invective ever published in America. It

was entitled *The Good Gray Poet,* and it told in remarkably effective rhetoric, the story of the outrage that was said to have been inflicted upon Walt as a penalty for having published a book that offended the puritanical Secretary of the Interior.

We must not fail to read this story in O'Connor's fiery and remarkably well-written narrative.

"On the 30th of last month, this true American man and author was dismissed, under circumstances of peculiar wrong, from a clerkship he had held for six months in the Department of the Interior. His dismissal was the act of Hon. James Harlan, the secretary of the Department, formerly a Methodist clergyman, and President of a Western College. Upon the interrogation of an eminent officer of the Government, at whose instance the appointment had, under a former Secretary, been made, Mr. Harlan averred that Walt Whitman had been in no way remiss in the discharge of his duties, but that, on the contrary, so far as he could learn, his conduct had been most exemplary. Indeed, during the few months of his tenure of office, he had been promoted. The sole and only cause of his dismissal, Mr. Harlan said, was that he had written a book of poetry entitled *Leaves of Grass.* This book Mr. Harlan characterized as 'full of indecent passages.' 'The author,' he said, was 'a very bad man' and a 'Free-Lover.' Argument being had on these propositions, Mr. Harlan was, as regards the book, utterly unable to maintain his assertions; and as regards the author, was forced to admit that his opinion of him had been changed. Nevertheless, after this substantial admission of his injustice, he absolutely refused to revoke his action. Of course, under no circumstances, would Walt Whitman, the proudest man that lives, have consented to again enter into office under Mr. Harlan; but the demand for his reinstatement was as honorable to the gentleman who made it as the refusal to accede to it was discreditable to the Secretary."

O'Connor then proceeded, with real ability as a writer, and an ardor that made his writing little less than eloquent even as it appears in print, to cite famous works of literature, by no means omitting the Bible, in which were found passages with which Whitman's alleged indecency might be compared. As he neared his peroration, O'Connor paused to admire his own calmness in the discussion. He darkly hinted that he knew facts which if he were to add them to the story of the dismissal would bring a storm of righteous indignation upon the head of the Secretary. He said:

It is with difficulty that I restrain my just indignation. Instead of my comparatively cold and sober treatment, this transaction deserves rather the pitiless exposure and the merciless, stern anger and red-hot steel scourge of Juvenal. But I leave untold its darkest details; and, waiving every other consideration, I rest solely and squarely on the general indignity this action offers to intellectual liberty. I claim that to expel an author from a public office and subject him to public contumely, solely because he has published a book which no one can declare immoral without declaring all the other great books immoral, is to affix a penalty to thought, and to obstruct the freedom of letters.

The "darkest details" which O'Connor skilfully kept in the background, because they were more effective thus obscurely hinted at, were not permanently kept in the shadow. They were that Harlan had not happened upon the book by accident, but had been told that Whitman was working on it in time paid for by the Government, and that it was an immoral book, and had himself borrowed it from Whitman's desk without permission and in Whitman's absence.

Whether Secretary Harlan was within his official rights in taking measures to learn what work a salaried clerk in his department was doing, and thus opening the desk and reading the book, I leave for others to discuss. The belief that Harlan did this was effectively hinted at by O'Connor, who knew better than to tell in plain language just how dark were the shocking details of Harlan's iniquity.[3]

If there is any man to whom Walt Whitman ought to have been sincerely grateful, it was to James Harlan. After the publication of O'Connor's vituperative tract,[4] few Secretaries would have dared to discharge Walt. He had abundant time to revise his *Leaves of Grass* at public expense.

It is much to Senator Harlan's credit that he bore this flood of criticism in dignified silence. Late in life as he was living in retirement, he received a courteous inquiry and once and for all he told his side of the story, but his letter has reached very few readers and it is hidden away in the appendix of his biography, published by the Iowa State Historical Society in 1913, thirty-eight years after the controversy. We shall do well to exhume it, and preserve it here:

Mt. Pleasant, Iowa,
July 18th, 1894.

Mr. Dewitt Miller,
Union League,
Philadelphia, Penn.
Dear Sir:—

I am in receipt of your letter of the 14th inst. requesting me to give you the reasons for the removal of the 1st Mr. Walt Whitman, in 1865, from a Clerkship in the office of the Commissioner of Indian Affairs, and the Department of the Interior.

You must pardon me for suggesting that it has not been usual for the heads of Departments of the National Government to assign to the public—nor to individuals for public use—their reasons for such official action. And that if they should so far forget the proprieties as to do so, such thoughtlessness would in many cases injure the reputation of the persons thus dropped from the public service, without being beneficial to any one. But in this case—impelled by a desire to gratify your wishes—I think I may so far depart from a commendable usage as to say generally that when I entered the Department of the Interior as its Chief, I found on its pay rolls a considerable number of useless incumbents who were seldom at their respective desks. Some of them were simply supernumerary, and some of them were worthless.

Deeming it my duty to administer the business of the Department economically as well as efficiently, I endeavored, with the aid of the heads of bureaus, to weed out the needless and worthless material.

Under this order, Mr. Walt Whitman, and a considerable number of others were, from time to time, removed, as the same were reported to me by their respective chiefs, for my action in the premises.

It would not be possible for me now, after the lapse of about twenty-nine years, to recall in detail the reasons reported to me by their respective heads of Bureaus, for their discontinuance in the public service, even if it were desirable and proper to recite them after many of them like Whitman have passed to the other side. It is, therefore, deemed needful only to say in relation to his removal, that his Chief—Hon. W. P. Dole, Commissioner of Indian Affairs, who was officially answerable to me for the work of his Bureau, recommended it, *on the ground that his services were not needed.* And no other reason was ever assigned by my authority.

You are kind enough to tell me that the reasons given for his dismissal by his friends are favorable to him and unfavorable to me.

I need only say on that point, that, according to my recollection, the same could be said truthfully of every one so removed by me during my incumbency of the office of Secretary. The least worthy usually raised the greatest clamor; making it clear to my mind that any one who would be seriously disturbed by such querulousness ought not to accept the position of the head of a Department, where he must necessarily perform such unpleasant duties.

> With great respect,
> Your obedient servant,
> JAS. HARLAN.

This letter, it will be noted, does not deny that Secretary Harlan read and disapproved *Leaves of*

Grass, and we must believe that this was true. But it gives a valid and unanswerable reason for Walt's discharge, and one that no friend of his has ever disputed, namely, that Whitman was not earning his salary by any work that he was doing for the Government.

I have made inquiry of the Department of the Interior in an effort to learn how many superfluous and incompetent clerks the Secretary discharged, and am informed that the Iowa Historical Society some years ago made the same inquiry; but the records covering the discharge of employees at that remote period are not accessible. It is evident, however, that there were many of them, not only a small army of clerks, but three department heads being among those dismissed. The Department of the Interior was in need of a thorough house-cleaning and got it. Walt could hardly have maintained his position even if he had been a Methodist. Indeed, it is highly probable that some Methodists were among those who lost their positions.

If the writing of a book which some people believe to be poetry and others classify as very dull prose, and some think indecent and others highly proper, entitles the author to a living without labor, there is no reason why those who think such a living deserved should not provide it out of their own pockets. There is not the slightest reason to doubt that Walt Whitman would have accepted such gratuity from them without a protest. But Walt's friends preferred that he should live at the charges of others, and that was equally acceptable to Walt provided he did not have to work. He got his job and his friends did not have to pay his salary. It was cheaper for them to howl about the bigotry of Harlan than to feed Walt. Meantime, several hundred people who had helped in the hospitals, possibly not as much as Walt, but at greater sacrifice, continued to work for their own living.

XI

WHEN THE CRUEL WAR WAS OVER

For the purpose of this narrative, the literary activity of Walt Whitman is divided into two parts by the death of Abraham Lincoln. In a subsequent chapter we shall sketch an outline of his literary development up to that event. Between *Leaves of Grass* and such of his early prose as may be regarded as literature, and that more spiritual interpretation of American life and thought which Whitman himself professed to intend to produce, his writings and utterances on Abraham Lincoln are, for our purposes, an important part. It will be convenient at this point to give a very brief outline of his life after the death of Lincoln. We shall later have occasion to go over his literary work as it related to Lincoln in approximately its chronological order, but we shall be able to do this with more freedom as to its literary expression if we have before our minds the order of events.

O'Connor sent his pamphlet, *The Good Gray Poet,* to George William Curtis, Ralph Waldo Emerson, Matthew Arnold and other eminent men on both sides of the Atlantic. It won for Walt a wide-spread sympathy and if anything had been needed to make his place secure, this would have accomplished the result. He now had a comfortable boarding place, a salary of sixteen hundred dollars a year, a desk at a great south window on the south side of the Treasury Building overlooking the Potomac and was allowed all the freedom he could desire. He established habits of reading which had not been conspicuous in him before. His desk was a much more comfortable place than his room in the boarding house, and he had a key which permitted him to go in and out at all hours. He wrote to his mother:

I go evenings up to the office frequently—I have got me a splendid astral lamp, to burn gas by a tube & it works to admiration (all at the expense of the office),—& there I can sit & read, &c, as nice as you please—then I am getting many books from the Library (our office Library) that I have long wanted to read at my leisure,—and can get any book I want in reason—so you can see it is a great privilege I have here.

When *Drum-Taps* was published, Horace E. Scudder, a Boston critic, sent a copy to W. M. Rossetti, and this resulted in articles published in England that began to give to Whitman that English recognition which has proved so remarkable an incident in the criticism of his work. Out of this grew his correspondence with Mrs. Anne Gilchrist who later came to America, somewhat to his embarrassment but also to his comfort. He had a letter also from Alfred Tennyson. He went forward in his literary work, notably that of his *Democratic Vistas* and his *Passage to India.* The latter, begun with a completion of the Suez Canal and the Pacific Railroad, opened in a very large way the promise of his undertaking a work on broadly prophetic lines as over against the more sensual aspects of *Leaves of Grass.*

In 1872 occurred his visit to Dartmouth College. This would appear to have been the result of a joke on the part of the students, but it was no joke to Walt. His commencement poem did not greatly thrill his auditors, but it delighted the college boys to know that they had been able to bring this result to pass, and it was a landmark in the literary experience of Walt Whitman.

The delightful group of companions, with whom Walt had enjoyed such fellowship in Washington, gradually disintegrated. Peter Doyle went to work for the Pennsylvania Railroad as a baggage master. John Burroughs bought his farm on the Hudson River and shook the dust of Washington and all other cities from his feet. With O'Connor, Walt's parting was tragic. That the two men should quarrel was inevitable, but the rift between them was so wide and the altercation so vehement that they parted violently asunder. After a long time they were reconciled, but the old quality of intimate friendship could never be restored.

In all these years no bezom of reform swept through the Department to trouble Walt's security. Andrew Johnson had followed Abraham Lincoln and he in turn was followed by General Grant, and it was not a time when reforms in the civil service made much progress. If Walt's health had not given way again, he might possibly have lived out a long life as a department clerk, and he had no higher political ambition.

We do not know the responsible cause of either of Walt's two physical breakdowns. The easy and popular explanation is that his hospital experience broke down his health. He himself was satisfied with this explanation. This may indeed have been a contributing cause. The malaria in the Washington climate was also recognized at the time as an important factor. That indeed appears to have been the diagnosis of at least one physician. Certainly Walt's habits with regard to diet and the lack of regular exercise may well have had their important effect. He was a flabby fat man who did nothing to harden his muscles or to keep down his excess of flesh. At intervals after his experience in 1864, he had what he called "spells in the head."

On January 23, 1873, he sat late by his astral lamp in the Treasury Department reading one of Bulwer-Lytton's novels. When he left at a late hour, the guard thought he looked ill. Between three and four the next morning, he woke to find himself paralyzed. For a few days it appeared that the attack might prove fatal. Then he began to rally, and by the end of March he was occasionally at his desk again.

Family sorrows brought him anxiety and grief. He was especially fond of Martha, the wife of his brother Jeff. She died that spring in St. Louis. On May twenty-third, he stood at the death-bed of his mother. She died at the home of his brother, George, in Camden, New Jersey. Whatever the faults of Walt Whitman, he had been a consistently affectionate son to his mother. Between him and his father apparently there had never been perfect sympathy, and his references to his father in his poems are not highly complimentary. But his devotion to his mother was sincere while she lived and his grief over her death was profound.

His brother George never had any very great sympathy for Walt. His career as a soldier was an honorable one and he stood well in business, but he never recognized Walt's writing as poetry and he had some justification in resenting Walt's indolence. He offered Walt a room in his house in Camden. Walt at first did not intend to accept, but he found himself unable to return to Washington. His hasty departure to the death-bed of his mother proved the final severing of his Washington relationship. His clerkship was kept open for him for a long time, but he never returned.

It is not to be supposed that Walt himself, after

long absence from the office, and with no prospect of recovery, voluntarily separated himself from the government pay-roll. As far as I am aware, no one hitherto has discovered just how his service as a department clerk finally ended. The following letter, now first published, will inform us of the manner in which, after more than seventeen months of absence, his position was lost:[1]

DEPARTMENT OF JUSTICE

Washington June 30, 1874.

Walt Whitman Esq.,
    Camden, N. J.,
Sir :-

Congress at its last session abolished one of the third-class clerkships in the office of the Solicitor of the Treasury, and upon my requesting the Solicitor to designate which of the three he could best dispense with, you were named. It is, therefore, my duty to inform you that your services will not be required from and after the first proximo.

I regret to have to send you this notice, but under the law limiting the force in the office the proposed reduction is necessary, and I do not feel at liberty to overrule the wishes of the Solicitor of the Treasury,

Very respectfully,
GEO. W. WILLIAMS.
Attorney General.

Walt was fifty-four and had nineteen years longer to live. He was not very happy under his brother's roof. He bought a cheap lot in a forlorn part of Camden and hoped for a time when he could build upon it. This hope was deferred, but in 1884 he purchased for seventeen hundred and fifty dollars a little two-story house at 328 Mickle Street.[2] He had nearly thirteen hundred dollars, the proceeds of his Philadelphia edition of *Leaves of Grass* printed in 1883. George W. Childs lent him the balance. It was an unattractive house in a slum district, near the railroad tracks and with unpleasant surroundings. A guano factory was not far away. The noise of the trains, and the smell of the factory troubled him less than they would have disturbed most men. The house had no furnace and was hard to heat in winter. It was insufferably hot in summer. Its ugliness and discomfort did not greatly trouble Walt. There was only one attractive thing about the place and that was a lilac bush in the back yard.

After some experiments a housekeeper was obtained, a plump widow, Mrs. Mary Davis. She admired poets even if she did not know much about their poetry. She sewed lace collars on Walt's shirts, thereby compensating for what she did not do with the broom and the scrubbing brush. Of her cooking, it need only be said that Walt made no complaint, which, however, is no very high compliment. The other living members of the household were a spotted dog, a black cat, a parrot and a canary.

Walt counted among Mrs. Davis' chief virtues

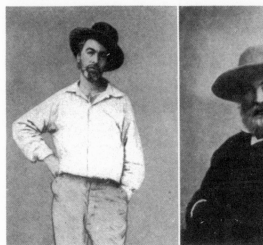

The Carpenter, 1855   The Hospital Visitor, 1863

The Departmental Clerk, 1867   The "Good Gray Poet," 1891

WALT WHITMAN

the fact that she seldom undertook to clean up his bedroom. He was welcome to litter as much as he pleased, and, sitting in his big chair, to poke around with his cane and pull his manuscripts to him as he wanted them. If his papers were too far away to be reached in that fashion, he could hobble around and find them or shout for Mrs. Davis. The chairs and tables in his room contained papers, manuscript, shoes, printer's proofs and unwashed dishes. There were trunks and boxes around the walls, and the bed stood in one corner, the linen not very clean and the bed was seldom made up. There was a sheet-iron air-tight stove and the poet could heat his room as red-hot as he pleased. It was Walt's idea of comfort.

To Mickle Street came an increasing group of younger men who admired Walt's poetry and wanted to meet the man. That wretched hovel became one of America's foremost literary shrines. Year by year Walt succeeded in publishing some of the things he wrote, and year by year he became a little more stout and flaccid. In December, 1891, he had pneumonia, which was followed by a general breaking-down. He died March 27, 1892, in his seventy-third year. To the surprise of his friends, who had contributed to his support, he left several thousand dollars in the bank, and by his direction, he was buried in a massive tomb which cost about four thousand dollars.

XII

LINCOLN AND WHITMAN

WE MAY now consider very briefly a few of the parallel events and qualities in the lives of Abraham Lincoln and Walt Whitman.[1]

Lincoln was born in 1809; Whitman ten years later in 1819. Lincoln died in 1865 at the age of fifty-six; Whitman died in 1892 aged nearly seventy-three. They were contemporaries for forty-six years from 1819 till 1865. Lincoln's months in the public schools were fewer than Whitman's, but Whitman left school at thirteen, while Lincoln's last experience in the school-room was when he was three or four years older. Whitman was beginning his career as a printer about the time Lincoln was doing his first surveying at New Salem. Lincoln was admitted to the bar in 1837, about the time Whitman was teaching school and boarding around.

Whitman began to edit the *Brooklyn Eagle* about the time that Lincoln was stumping his congressional district and winning his way into Congress, serving there in 1848-49.

Whitman's journey down the Mississippi to New Orleans occurred in 1848, seventeen years after Lincoln's second and more memorable voyage to that city. But Whitman, making his way north and east after his experience in New Orleans, and traveling by way of Chicago, might have encountered somewhere about the St. Clair Flats or at Buffalo, Abraham Lincoln, returning from his one term in Congress and from his visit to New England where he had been speaking on behalf of General Taylor, Whig candidate for the Presidency. If these two men had met at Niagara Falls, it would have been interesting to know what they would have said to each other. We know what each of them said about the Falls. They did not meet there, and they never met afterward.

Each of these two men was a carpenter's son, and each of them served something of an apprenticeship at that trade.

Lincoln's mother died early and his father lived until Lincoln had been in Congress. Whitman's mother survived his father, and lived almost as long as Walt himself. Both men felt permanently the influence of the mother as an important factor in their lives.

At thirty, Whitman was in Brooklyn, out of employment, and without a definite purpose in life. At thirty, Abraham Lincoln was in the early years of his experience in Springfield, making less than a living, and with his future obscure.

Both Lincoln and Whitman inherited the Democratic type of political faith. Lincoln early broke with his antecedents and became a Whig, and in 1856 a Republican. Whitman became a Republican in the same year, but had his approach through the Free Soil movement. Neither of them was an enthusiastic abolitionist, but each was a friend of freedom and a lover of the Union.

Lincoln arrived in Washington in February, 1861, as President-elect of the United States, and resided there until his death, April 15, 1865. Whitman reached Washington at the end of December, 1862, and resided there until May, 1873. They were contemporaries in that city from the closing days of 1862 until April, 1865.

Thus, with all brevity, we recall the parallel events in the lives of Lincoln and Whitman, and the dates of some of the main events of Walt Whitman's life, after Lincoln's death. There remain for us a few chapters of Whitman's life, as they relate to his interpretation of Abraham Lincoln.

Walt Whitman wrote nothing about Abraham Lincoln for publication while Lincoln was alive. After Lincoln was dead, it was a long time before very many people cared whether he said anything about Lincoln or if so, what it was he said. Collections of poetry concerning Lincoln began to be made quite early. Late in 1874, Ralph Waldo Emerson published an anthology of poems of his own selection. The volume was entitled

Parnassus. That volume does not contain one poem by Walt Whitman about Lincoln or anything else. Very tardily and with great reluctance and much hesitation he was admitted to be a poet. One of his poems gradually gained a degree of popularity and that was one which related to Lincoln.

Before Walt became an interpreter of Lincoln he was interpreting America. It would be too much to say that he ever made a systematic plan, yet roughly he appears to have had a vague idea of interpreting America in its material resources in his earlier writings, and then to have conceived the plan of another interpretation in aspects more nearly spiritual. In the preface to his first edition of *Leaves of Grass* in 1855, he said: "The Americans of all nations at any time upon the earth, have probably the fullest poetical nature. The United States themselves are essentially the greatest poem." He thought of America itself as a song. Not in his first edition, but in that of 1860, he wrote:

I HEAR AMERICA SINGING

I hear America singing, the varied carols I hear,
Those of mechanics, each one singing his as it should be blithe and strong,
The carpenter singing his as he measures his plank or beam,
The mason singing his as he makes ready for work, or leaves off work,

The boatman singing what belongs to him in his boat, the
      deckhand singing on the steamboat deck,
The shoemaker singing as he sits on his bench, the hatter
      singing as he stands,
The wood-cutter's song, the ploughboy's on his way in
      the morning, or at noon intermission or at sun-
      down,
The delicious singing of the mother, or of the young
      wife at work, or of the girl sewing or washing,
Each singing what belongs to him or her and to none else,
The day what belongs to the day—at night the party of
      young fellows, robust, friendly,
Singing with open mouths their strong melodious songs.

The opening poem of his first edition became one
of his most familiar utterances, and it excited many
derisive comments:

I celebrate myself, and sing myself,
And what I assume you shall assume,
For every atom belonging to me as good belongs to you.

I loaf and invite my soul,
I lean and loaf at ease, observing a spear of summer grass.

That Walt was a colossal egotist no one has ever
dreamed of denying, but this utterance was not
wholly egotism. It was the acclamation of personality. His whole book was the incarnation of
a personal spirit—his own spirit and the spirit
which he believed to be that of America. He could
say in truth:

Camerado, this is no book,
Who touches this touches a man.

The soul of America to Walt Whitman was a personal soul. It did not interpret itself to him wholly in mountains and rivers and continental vistas and occupation, nor yet in quantity production. His was the glory of personality, and it is to Whitman's enduring honor that he infused the element of personality as an essential ingredient into the interpretation of America. He said:

I swear I begin to see the meaning of these things,
It is not the earth, it is not America who is so great,
It is I who am great and to be great, it is You up there,
    or any one,
It is to walk rapidly through civilizations, governments,
    theories,
Through poems, pageants, shows, to form individuals.

Underneath all, individuals,
I swear nothing is good to. me now that ignores
    individuals,
The American compact is altogether with individuals,
The whole government is that which makes minute of
    individuals,
The whole theory of the universe is directed unerringly
    to one single individual—namely to You.

The war gave a new and solemn aspect to these visions of vastness and power. He saw very little of battle-fields, but he beheld much of their result. What he beheld of carnage left its mark upon his memory and he sought for the deeper meaning of this tragedy in the birth-pangs of freedom, and day and night he dreamed about it.

In midnight sleep of many a face of anguish,
Of the look at first of the mortally wounded, (of that
    indescribable look,)
Of the dead on their backs with arms extended wide,
    I dream, I dream, I dream.

Of scenes of Nature, fields and mountains,
Of skies so beauteous after a storm, and at night the
    moon so unearthly bright,
Shining sweetly, shining down, where we dig the trenches
    and gather the heaps,
    I dream, I dream, I dream.

Long have they pass'd, faces and trenches and fields,
Where through the carnage I moved with a callous com-
    posure, or away from the fallen,
Onward I sped at the time—but now of their forms at
    night,
    I dream, I dream, I dream.

To say that he planned his later work as an effort to give expression to the spiritual side of American progress would be to impute to Walt a much more definite and deliberate purpose than that of which he was conscious, but some adumbration of a purpose akin to this he had. He saw America on its open road discovering new avenues of progress, and they were not wholly material. His poem on Columbus was really but a mask for his own spirit in the interpretation of American life. In 1876, commenting on his *Passage to India,* he said that it had been his intention, after chanting in *Leaves of Grass* the songs of the body and existence, "to compose a further and equally needed volume, based on those convictions of perpetuity and conservation which, enveloping all precedents, make the unseen soul govern absolutely at last." This was to have involved in completion what he found himself able at best to adumbrate, and that only in fragments, thoughts "on death, immortality, and a free entrance into the spiritual world." Had he been able to complete his interpretation, we are assured that it would not have been in terms of bulk and production, but in values of spiritual quest and vision. With him, in its aspiration after spiritual certainty and assurance of high destiny, America cries, and the world cries:

O give me the clew; It lurks in the night here somewhere,
O if I am to have so much, let me have more!

Had he lived to carry out this purpose, and living had remembered to fulfill it, we might have other poems than those he left on the more spiritual aspects of America's mission, and perhaps more about Lincoln.

To him, modernity was not decadence. As his years advanced and he saw strange portents and could not understand their meaning, he assured himself that humanity was coming to its own through the inner meanings of material accomplishments:

Years of the modern! years of the unperform'd!
Your horizon rises, I see it parting away for more august
    dramas,
I see not America only, not only Liberty's nation but
    other nations preparing,
I see tremendous entrances and exits, new combinations,
    the solidarity of races,
I see that force advancing with irresistible power on the
    world's stage,
(Have the old forces, the old wars, played their parts?
    are the acts suitable to them closed?)
I see Freedom, completely arm'd and victorious and very
    haughty, with Law on one side and Peace on the
    other,
A stupendous trio all issuing forth against the idea of
    caste;
What historic denouements are these we so rapidly ap-
    proach?
I see men marching and countermarching by swift
    millions,
I see frontiers and boundaries of the old aristocracies
    broken,
I see the landmarks of European kings removed,
I see this day the People beginning their landmarks (all
    others give way);
Never were such sharp questions ask'd as this day,
Never was average man, his soul, more energetic, more
    like a God,
Lo, how he urges and urges, leaving the masses no rest!
His daring foot is on land and sea everywhere, he
    colonizes the Pacific, the archipelagoes,

With the steamship, the electric telegraph, the newspaper,
    the wholesale engines of war,
With these and the world spreading factories he inter-
    links all geography, all lands;
What whispers are these O lands, running ahead of you,
    passing under the seas?
Are all nations communing? is there going to be but one
    heart to the globe?
Is humanity forming en-masse? for lo, tyrants tremble,
    crowns grow dim,
The earth restive, confronts a new era, perhaps a general
    divine war,
No one knows what will happen next, such portents fill the
    days and nights;
Years prophetical! the space ahead as I walk, as I vainly
    try to pierce it, full of phantoms,
Unborn deeds, things soon to be, project their shapes
    around me,
This incredible rush and heat, this strange ecstatic fever
    of dreams O years!
Your dreams O years, how they penetrate through me!
    (I know not whether I sleep or wake);
The perform'd America and Europe grow dim, retiring
    in shadow behind me,
The unperform'd, more gigantic than ever, advance, ad-
    vance upon me.

Thus it came about after the Civil War with its
back-wash of disillusionment and misgovernment
which did not seriously disturb Walt, that he found
a larger meaning in that first literary purpose
which he published in 1855 in the preface to
Leaves of Grass, namely: "to express in literary
and poetic form, and uncompromisingly, my own

emotional, moral, intellectual and æsthetic Personality, in the midst of, and tallying, the momentous spirit and facts of immediate days, and of current America—and to exploit that personality, identified with place and date, in a far more candid and comprehensive sense than any hitherto poem or book."

Whitman saw very little of America. He made but two journeys of importance, one to New Orleans in his young manhood and one later to St. Louis and the nearer reaches of the Rocky Mountains. His life was spent in Brooklyn, Washington and Camden. With those cities as cities he had very little to do, nor had he much to do with any other cities or places. Yet he felt that America was his. In a very real sense he was right. In his big, indistinct but effective vision, he discovered the spirit of America animating and motivating the forms of its material development. He interpreted America in terms of personality.

This brought him inevitably to Abraham Lincoln. Lincoln, whom he thought of during Lincoln's life-time as a giant "Westerner," the representative of a section of America, he came to discover as a personal incarnation of the very life and spirit of America. In this discovery of the soul of Lincoln the soul of Walt Whitman may almost be said to have a new birth.

Walt Whitman saw very little of Abraham Lincoln, and his glimpses were not very significant.

He was never present on any great occasion when Lincoln did any notable thing. And Lincoln saw nothing of Whitman. Virtually they were strangers to each other. Yet Whitman felt that Lincoln was akin to him. He said that Lincoln "particularly belonged" to him. Emerson said very nearly the same thing about Carlyle. When the Concord philosopher's mind had become clouded and he failed to recognize his friends or to recall their names, he looked at Carlyle's portrait hanging in his room, and, unable to remember just what it was that bound him to Carlyle, said, "He's my man." Whitman felt that way about Lincoln. Emerson had introduced Carlyle to his American readers; Carlyle was indeed his man. Whitman had rendered no such service to Lincoln; yet he felt that Lincoln was his.

Strangely, and yet with reason, the literary world has accepted Whitman as an interpreter of Lincoln and of the spirit of America. What had these two men in common, and in what did they differ?

In some respects their minds were quite unlike. Lincoln was analytical and logical; Whitman was synthetic and miscellaneous. Lincoln used simple language, and employed his words with an accurate sense of their value; Whitman was fond of large, mouth-filling phrases, and was seldom over-precise as to their definition. Lincoln used forth-right Saxon speech; Whitman, proud as he was of being an American, had an affectation for foreign phrases which he did not always use correctly. Lincoln resolved ideas into their component elements; Whitman was fond of intellectual bulk. Lincoln's mind moved under the perception of cause and effect; Whitman's moved under the impact of mass.

Both Lincoln and Whitman were men of large self-confidence; but Lincoln's self-esteem was chastened by a manifest modesty. Whitman possessed a rude intellectual arrogance. One of his most discriminating biographers says that Whitman could not understand how a man could be a gentleman without ceasing to be a man.

Whitman lacked a sense of humor; one of his biographers says of him that if any one had told him that he was a greater man than Shakespeare, "he would have accepted the compliment and never turned a hair." Lincoln, on the other hand, had a keen sense of humor, and a large appreciation of the ridiculous.

There were traits which they had in common, and these were not less pronounced than those in which they differed.

Each was a man of powerful physique, and each was disinclined to physical labor. Each had a slow-moving mind. Neither was given to jumping to conclusions, or committing hasty actions. But though Lincoln did not love work, he worked, which was a difference between him and Whitman.

Whitman was descended from a Quaker family, and Lincoln believed himself so to have descended. Each had some of the characteristics usually associated with those of members of the Society of Friends. Each had respect for that body and a certain pride in having his supposed inheritance known. Neither of these two men, however, was an adherent of that sect. Each was profoundly a lover of peace, and a man of unusual sympathy. Both were moody, Whitman at times with a sullen silence, and Lincoln with a woe too deep for words.

Each of these two men was ambitious, and that to an unusual degree. Each had an estimate of his own powers that led him to undertake for himself and to demand from others recognitions almost staggeringly great. Each dearly loved publicity, and liked to hear himself praised.

Each of these two men had strong passions, and full capacity for procreation, but each shrank from marriage. Lincoln's shrinking may have been based in part upon the social disparity between him and the women he loved, but other men have encountered greater disparity and have overcome it. Lincoln had some deeper and as yet unexplained reason for his strange conduct in the matter of his courtships. Whitman gave as his reason for not marrying, "I had an instinct against forming ties that would bind me." Lincoln married and became the father of children. Whitman became the father of children, but did not marry.

Each of these two men had in him an element which was nothing short of Rabelaisian, yet each had his standard of morality. It was not the same standard, but each of them had it.

Each of these two men had to wait until after his death for an adequate recognition of his work. Each while living was derided and condemned.

Lincoln was nothing if not honest. Yet his honesty was accompanied by an element of adroitness which caused him to be accused of "low cunning." If I say that Whitman, too, was honest, I shall seem to contradict much that is most certainly true about him. He was not invariably truthful; his egoism and lack of any sense of the absurd as it related to his own sense of greatness made him incapable of exact truthfulness, and that is not the worst that must be admitted about him. He accepted from those who were ready to serve him such as they had to give, and did not give his confidence or his good faith in equal measure. He accepted from women what women had to give, and presumably were glad to give, and he denied them any reciprocal bestowal of protection. He permitted his friends to deny on his behalf charges that he knew to be true, and concerning which they unwittingly falsified themselves in his interest and with his knowledge.[2]

Lincoln was almost incapable of lying. Whitman prevaricated very easily. A man can lie and not be a liar; and some men more than others. If

I were to say that Whitman lied habitually and yet that he was not quite a liar, I should certainly be misunderstood, but I should not need to say with Walt what "I probably mean." I certainly do not mean that he was too moral to lie. I could rather say that he was too a-moral. Walt did not, like Lincoln, strip a proposition of all its unessential qualities and compel it to stand forth naked and unashamed; he saw truths in vague, indistinct bulks shrouded in intellectual and ethical lack of precision. In the face of all this and more it requires some courage to affirm that Walt Whitman had in him a real basis of sturdy honesty, not wholly unlike that of Abraham Lincoln. In his egregious self-esteem, his insatiable love of posing, his indolent willingness to accept charity rather than work, he was not honest: but there was in him a basic loyalty to his convictions, whatever those convictions may have been, a quality that forbids us to think of him as intrinsically dishonest. The lantern of Diogenes is none too bright to discover and classify honest men. There is said to be honor among thieves, and of some men who are worse it may be said:

> His honor rooted in dishonor stood,
> And faith unfaithful kept him falsely true.

This, however, was not the case with Whitman. He glorified his own doings, and perhaps gloried in his shame, but these were not his dominant qualities.   They were eddies and cross-currents in a channel whose deeper flow was honest.

The bluff frankness of Whitman, the hearty and humorous salutation of Lincoln, sent men away thinking that they had looked into the very heart of the man whom they addressed.   In each case the depths of the heart were unplumbed.   Both Whitman and Lincoln were by nature secretive to an extreme; yet each had the faculty of seeming to take a casual acquaintance completely into his confidence.   Neither of them wore his heart upon his sleeve.   Each kept his own counsel, and was capable of keeping it while learning other men's minds and secreting his own.

Each of these two men, and these beyond all other men of their generation, interpreted the spirit of America to the world.   There is this marked difference, that the common people understood Lincoln and never understood Whitman.   The people who accept Whitman's democracy are the intellectual aristocrats, the alleged "high-brows" and not the common people.   The common people have never cared for Whitman, and there is no present prospect that they ever will.   But they understand and love Lincoln.   Yet if the common American citizen is content to let Whitman "hurl his barbaric yawp over the roofs of the world," as he said he did, and as he did, the world at large interprets America in the spirit of Whitman.

Lincoln not only believed in the common people,

but the common people believed in him and in his
theories of democracy.   Whitman believed in the
common people, but the common people have never
cared for Whitman.   This is the pathetic fact about
the poetry of Whitman, that while it is written to
express the spirit of the common people, it is held
in honor by aristocrats and men and women who
affect a pose, and people of whom Whitman took
little heed.

Emerson wrote to Carlyle in 1856:

> One book, last summer, came out in New York, a
> nondescript monster, which yet had terrible eyes and
> buffalo strength, and was indisputably American—which
> I thought to send you; but the book throve so badly with
> the few to whom I showed it, and wanted good morals so
> much, that I never did.   Yet I believe now again I shall.

That was an apt description.   It had terrible
eyes and buffalo strength, and was indisputably
American.   Whitman knew of what sort he was:

> Bearded, gray-necked, sunburnt, forbidding, I have
>   arrived,
> To be wrestled with as I pass for the solid prizes of the
>   universe.

Whitman was primarily a democrat.   He cele-
brated himself, his own convictions, his own whims,
his own country.   He was a turbulent spirit, big,
bulky, belligerent.   Close to the Civil War as he
was, he never saw a battle, but his life was a loafing
battle for his own convictions, a leisurely fight for

what he believed to be the right. It was funda-
mentally a fight for freedom, and he believed it
was a fight for the spirit of democracy as it existed
in America.

Neither Lincoln nor Whitman saw very much of
America. Each journeyed to New Orleans, and
each saw Niagara Falls. Each had a notable trip
west of the Mississippi, but did not penetrate to the
coast. Whitman had his Dartmouth College invitation, and Lincoln his Cooper Union address, and
his two tours of New England, but each was a
stranger to the culture of the East. Although
Whitman was born on Long Island and died in
Camden, his thoughts were of the interior: he saw
little of the great nation but his feelings were
national. Lincoln, whose whole life until his election as President was spent in the interior, and
rather close to the fringes of civilization, was
national in his outlook, and believed in a house
not divided against itself.

These are the two men of whom the world thinks
and often thinks simultaneously when it endeavors
to understand the meaning and message of
America. In Whitman they discover, or think
they do, its boisterous, enterprising spirit of self-
assertion and of conscious power, its disregard of
precedent, its courage to be and to celebrate itself.
In Lincoln they discover, or think they do, the
type of citizenship and of leadership which may be
produced by a republic at its best.

These two men, whatever else may be said of them, learned to think nationally, and the world interprets them as exponents of the spirit of the nation in whose life they were contemporaries. We can think of many differences between them, which might prevent their classification together; but the two names insistently rearrange themselves; the world has come to think of Lincoln and Whitman as the two foremost interpreters of the spirit of America.

Both Lincoln and Whitman had early aspirations after a career on the public platform. Lincoln, after his debates with Douglas, having won a considerable repute in that contest without having received any reward in the way of office, thought to turn his publicity to good account by lecturing. He prepared a lecture on *Discoveries and Inventions* which he delivered in a number of towns in Illinois in 1859, but he was not a success as a lecturer, and soon gave up the attempt and did not renew it. Whitman began earlier, tried oftener, and in his later years delivered, once a year, a lecture of which more is to be said in a later chapter.

Both Lincoln and Whitman had in them youthful ambition and a measure of precocity. Each began early at a number of experiments. That in both cases the experiments failed is not enough to distinguish them. A very large proportion of American business men fail. But those who fail at one thing often succeed in another, and this was true of both of the men.

What is more significant, however, is that each of these men had that adult enlightenment, that time of self-discovery, which has characterized most of the founders of religions and the men who have established notable institutions. Mohammed, Buddha, John the Baptist, Francis of Assissi, Martin Luther and other men who have made history have had this experience. It came to Whitman after many failures and partial successes; it came to Lincoln and changed him, a man of integrity and ability, from a politician to a statesman. Some men know the day and hour when this illumination comes to them. In some lives the moment is indubitably distinguishable. In others it is less easily located, but no less certainly evident. In religion it is called the new birth. By whatever name it is known, its psychological significance is notable. Lincoln and Whitman were in this sense, and each in his relation to his own life-work, twice-born men.

There was in both Lincoln and Whitman something of the spirit which no other term can describe than the word "prophetic." That is not the ability to make shrewd guesses at incidents and events in the days to come; it is an ability to interpret the present so that therein the destiny of the future shall be revealed. Lincoln knew this quality, and realized it in himself, when he planted his feet firmly on the conviction that America could not permanently endure half slave and half free. Whitman felt it in the immensity of America's life, and the struggle out of which was to come her contribution to the life of the world.

To each of these two men, Abraham Lincoln and Walt Whitman, was given a vision of the ampler frontiers of the American ideal. Each of them discerned something of this wider significance of American freedom. It was not identical with the conception which the founders of the republic had; they were mainly concerned with what was in the foreground, political freedom from foreign rule. The older generations sang:

> Let independence be your boast,
> Ever mindful what it cost.

Lincoln and Whitman were mindful of that cost, but that was not the measure of their thought of independence. They were more mindful of what independence might procure. Walt wrote first, and last a number of poems entitled *Thought* or *Thoughts*. Not every one of them was as thoughtful as it might have been. But one of them, marred by mannerisms, has in a part of it that rare quality which Whitman possessed at his best. He was writing of America, and in lines nothing less than prophetic he said:

Of these years I sing,
How they pass and have pass'd through convuls'd pains,
    as through parturitions,

How America illustrates birth, muscular youth, the
      promise, the sure fulfilment, the absolute success,
      despite of people—illustrates evil as well as good,
The vehement struggle so fierce for unity in one's-self;
How many hold despairingly yet to the models departed,
      caste, myths, obedience, compulsion, and to
      infidelity,
How few see the arrived models, the athletes, the Western
      States, or see freedom or spirituality, or hold any
      faith in results,
(But I see the athletes, and I see the results of the war
      glorious and inevitable, and they again leading to
      other results.)

How the great cities appear—how the Democratic
      masses, turbulent, wilful, as I love them,
How the whirl, the contest, the wrestle of evil with good,
      the sounding and resounding, keep on and on,
How society waits unform'd, and is for a while between
      things ended and things begun,
How America is the continent of glories, and of the
      triumph of freedom and of the Democracies, and
      of the fruits of society and of all that is begun,
And how the States are complete in themselves—and how
      all triumphs and glories are complete in them-
      selves, to lead onward,
And how these of mine and of the States will in their turn
      be convuls'd, and serve other parturitions and
      transitions,
And how all people, sights, combinations, the democratic
      masses too, serve—and how every fact, and war
      itself, with all its horrors, serves,
And how now or at any time each serves the exquisite
      transition of death.

Walt came of a family that was deeply rooted in Long Island soil, and which had not adventured far. But in him was a quality that was his very own, and was also the very heart and soul of America, and preeminently the spirit of Lincoln, the quality that gives essential character to the spirit of the pioneer:

>   Have the elder races halted?
> Do they droop and end their lesson, wearied over there
>   beyond the seas?
> We take up the task eternal, and the burden and the
>   lesson,
>   Pioneers! O pioneers!
>
>   All the past we leave behind,
> We debouch upon a newer, mightier world, varied world,
> Fresh and strong the world we seize, world of labor and
>   the march,
>   Pioneers! O pioneers!
>
>   We detachments steady throwing,
> Down the edges, through the passes, up the mountains
>   steep,
> Conquering, holding, daring, venturing as we go the un-
>   known ways,
>   Pioneers! O pioneers!
>
>   We primeval forests felling,
> We the rivers stemming, vexing we and piercing deep the
>   mines within,
> We the surface broad surveying, we the virgin soil up-
>   heaving,
>   Pioneers! O pioneers!

On and on the compact ranks,
With accessions ever waiting, with the places of the dead
quickly fill'd,
Through the battle, through defeat, moving yet and never
stopping,
Pioneers! O pioneers!

O to die advancing on!
Are there some of us to droop and die? has the hour come?
Then upon the march we fittest die, soon and sure the gap
is fill'd,
Pioneers! O pioneers!

All the pulses of the world,
Falling in they beat for us, with the Western movement
beat,
Holding single or together, steady moving to the front,
all for us,
Pioneers! O pioneers!

Nor was their idea of freedom identical with that
of the abolitionist, though each desired the freedom
of all men. To each was granted the vision of a
continent inhabited by men emancipated from
traditions of older and wearied nations. Lincoln
discerned this ideal in terms of more precise thinking and accurate definition; Whitman beheld it dim
in outline but vast and impressive in bulk. Lincoln
thought of it in carefully formulated propositions
of a government of, by and for the people; Whitman felt rather than saw the birth-agonies of a
vast and compelling national life. It was of

Columbus he professed to write, but the things he
described were those he himself saw:

Is it the prophet's thought I speak, or am I raving?
What do I know of life? What of myself?
I know not even my own work past or present,
Dim ever—shifty guesses of it spread before me,
Of newer, better worlds, their mighty parturition,
Mocking, perplexing me.

And these things I see suddenly, what mean they?
As if some miracle, some hand divine, unseal'd my eyes?
Shadowy vast ships smile through the air and sky,
As on the distant waves sail countless ships,
And anthems in new tongue I hear saluting me.

Both Lincoln and Whitman thought of the
history of his country as sacred. Neither of them
could have listened with patience to a languid discussion of the justice of the principles underlying
the American Revolution, or the righteousness
that animated the men who fought with Washington for liberty. Either of them would have admitted the existence of elements of selfishness
which marred the beginnings of America's national
existence, and which still halt its progress and cloud
its hope of the future. But each believed in the
sanity and justice of the ideal which on this virgin
continent brought forth and cradled a new nation,
struggling to free itself and the world from the
thousand evils that had sheltered themselves behind
the thrones of kings.

The glory which a religionist discovers in the Church, its fostering of learning, its cradling of art, its enshrinement in noblest architecture, its solemn and reverberating music, these two men, whose interest and action fell within another and a kindred sphere, discovered in the nation. They were right in their discovery. If the State be on the one hand only a visible expression in terms of political and military development of human genius for organization, it is on the other hand expression of the divine will. A righteous government the world has yet to see. It has been slow to come, and has not altogether come, in the Church. It will not come there until it comes also in the State.

Something of this conviction was in the mind of these two men, and the State, as they saw it, was America, a state in which the will of God was to be expressed in the intelligent and righteous will of a people made capable of governing themselves, and showing an example to the world. Nothing less than this was in the thought of both these two exponents of America's democracy, and nothing short of this will permanently satisfy the American ideal either in religion or in politics.

Both of these two men hated robbery, tyranny, injustice and oppression. Both loved liberty, and their faith in it was the basis of their creed in human government. To each of them freedom was something to be loved with a passionate devotion. A

government conceived in liberty and dedicated to
the ideal of equality before the law was more than
a form of administration—it was a religion.
Democracy was to them not merely a form of
political organization, but a philosophy of life.

And so each of them in his own way gloried in
the ideal of America, and each in a measure made
his personality the incarnation of his ideal. Each
lived and moved and had his being in the large free
spirit of America's inspiring hope of freedom.
Each believed in it as his country's unique and
largest gift to humanity. Each believed, as
Lincoln said, that in America we were either to
perpetuate and disseminate this ideal, or in the loss
of it, through infidelity to our divinely commis-
sioned duty, to lose it for ourselves and posterity
and the whole of humanity. Both believed what
Lincoln said, that we would either nobly save or
meanly lose the last best home of mankind.

Two men believing less ardently than they believed in democracy could not have said what they
said or hoped as they hoped for the triumph of the
democratic ideal. No tepid judgment that on the
whole democracy was better than other forms of
government would have sufficed for either Whitman or Lincoln. Each had to believe and each
did believe that America in geographic bulk, in
diversity of soil, climate and product, in tolerance
and open-mindedness, in opportunity to think and
plan and expand and achieve, in liberty to bargain

and experiment and blunder and discuss and build, was developing an ardent devotion to an ennobling ideal, and a mission to humanity that was more than prophetic, was truly Messianic. Each believed that the Spirit of the Lord was upon this country, and that this nation was anointed to proclaim liberty to them that were bruised, to open blind eyes, to bring the oppressed out of the prison house, and to preach an acceptable new era of the Lord.

Lincoln was not the only statesman, and Whitman was not the only poet to whom America was sacred as the incarnation of the ideal of freedom. Statesmen there had been from Patrick Henry and Richard Henry Lee and old Sam Adams who had proclaimed it. Poets there had been, and poets there were, who sang of it. Lowell in his *Biglow Papers* and his *Present Crisis,* Whittier from his soldier's heart that sang beneath a Quaker's coat, and Emerson in his *Concord Hymn* and later in his *Boston Hymn* sang their songs of freedom. Yet there was that in Whitman, as there was in Lincoln, in physical bulk and stature, in intellectual development and schooling close to the soil, in temperament and training, and in the whole complex of their personalities, which made them especial prophets of the progress of liberty, and champions of the rights of men.

They sang their songs and wrought their deeds and uttered their prophetic affirmations, not in isolation, but each of them in a preeminent perception of something in American life and hope which they saw clearer or held dearer or defined more adequately than most other men.

Orators are accustomed to glorify the ideal of free government. One might adduce sentences from Demosthenes on *The Crown* or from Cicero's orations against Cataline, and from men in every century since, who spoke with a growing appreciation of such freedom as was known when Greece nurtured ideals of liberty. In the days when to be a Roman was greater than to be a king, inspiring conceptions of liberty were ventured and honored. Browning, in his *Lost Leader,* remembering when Wordsworth had worn the red shirt of revolution in France, but later had settled down into a quiet recipient of a stipend from the Government, could call, and did call, a roll of poets who loved freedom. Browning could sing vehemently:

Shakespeare was of us, Milton was for us,
　Burns, Shelley, were with us,—they watch from their
　　graves!
He alone breaks from the van and the freemen:
　—He alone sinks to the rear and the slaves!

Poets and orators have been friends of freedom in many generations. But this orator and this poet, this raw-boned Abraham Lincoln, and the big, swaggering Walt Whitman, have become preeminently the spokesmen for that type of freedom which America has given to the world in political and spiritual idealism.

When Walt wrote his poem *Miracles* he apparently did not think of America in its entirety as something that he might properly mention. He concerned himself with details in human life and in the aspects of nature. But I am confident that if any one had said to him that it was common in ancient nations for each country to think of itself as having been guided toward a destiny that showed the purpose and pleasure of its deity, and that this had been preeminently true of the people out of whose national life the Bible grew, Walt would have declared, and I think rightly, that if any nation had a right to make that claim, America had that right. He might or might not have added a stanza to his poem; it is too late to add it now; but one can easily see where Whitman might have said that America was not only a poem, but also a miracle. Here is the poem:

Why, who makes much of a miracle?
As to me, I know of nothing else but miracles,
Whether I walk the streets of Manhattan,
Or dart my sight over the roofs of houses toward the sky,
Or wade with naked feet along the beach just in the edge
    of the water,
Or stand under trees in the woods,
Or talk by day with anyone I love, or sleep in the bed at
    night with anyone I love,
Or sit at table at dinner with the rest,

Or look at strangers opposite me riding in the car,
Or watch honey-bees busy around the hive of a summer
     forenoon,
Or animals feeding in the fields,
Or birds, or the wonderfulness of insects in the air,
Or the wonderfulness of sundown, or of stars shining so
     quiet and bright,
Or the exquisite thin curve of the new moon in spring;
These with the rest, one and all are to me miracles,
The whole referring, yet each distinct and in its place.
To me every hour of the light and dark is a miracle,
Every cubic inch of space is a miracle.
Every square yard of the surface of the earth is spread
     with the same,
Every foot of the interior swarms with the same.

To me the sea is a continual miracle,
The fishes that swim—the rocks—the motion of the
     waves—the ships with men in them,
What stranger miracles are there?

XIII

As THE Civil War receded, and some of its heroes sank into obscurity but its major characters advanced to new elevations in popular appreciation, it became almost if not quite inevitable that Walt Whitman should have come to think and speak increasingly of Lincoln. As Lincoln grew in fame and honor, and men who had known him grew less numerous, it became increasingly natural for Walt in his conversation and his writings to mention Lincoln in terms of growing intimacy and appreciation.

At Whitman's home in Camden, Lincoln was a frequent topic of conversations. Almost every visitor spoke of Whitman's poems on Lincoln, or of Whitman's having seen Lincoln. Whitman himself often introduced the subject. The three Boswellian volumes of Horace Traubel, (and there are in manuscript other volumes as yet unpublished) give us many incidental allusions to Lincoln in the conversations of Whitman, but nothing whatever that adds to our material concerning Whit-

166

man's real knowledge of the living Lincoln.[1] Whitman answered direct questions briefly, and soon fell into generalizations, as on November 11, 1888:

We talked of Lincoln; "What was your first impression of Lincoln?" W.: "I did not enthuse at the beginning, but I made up what I may call a prophetic judgment from things I heard of him: facts, stories, lights that came in my way. Lincoln's composure was marvellous: he was self-contained—had a thorough grip on himself. For two or three years he was generally regarded darkly, scornfully, suspiciously, in Washington, through the North."

There is not much original information in this, except the fact that Whitman did not immediately realize the greatness of Lincoln, and that he obtained his knowledge of Lincoln from others.

Whitman spoke often of Lincoln's portrait, which hung in his room, and to which he and his friends drank toasts and addressed remarks. He maintained that there never had been a really good portrait of Lincoln: but he counted best the one which he lent to the *North American Review,* and which is printed in his article on Lincoln.[2] Whitman declared that the photograph which he lent for this purpose was never returned to him, and that it was the best portrait of Lincoln ever made. It was Brady's standing portrait, with one arm behind the back. Traubel says:

W. talked humorously of portraits, of traditions about public men. "I meet new Walt Whitmans every day.

There are a dozen of me afloat. I don't know which Walt Whitman I am. Now there's Abraham Lincoln: people get to know his traits, his habits of life, some of his characteristics set off in the most positive relief: soon all sorts of stories are fathered off on him—some of them true, some of them apocryphal—volumes of stories (stories decent and indecent) fathered on him: legitimate stories, illegitimate: and so Lincoln comes to us more or less falsified. Yet I know that the hero is after all greater than any idealization."[3]

Whitman was often addressed as if he had sustained intimate relations with Lincoln, and it would not always have been easy for him to deny that it had been so. Donaldson,[4] says:

At the dinner given to Mr. Whitman by his personal friends in 1890, May 31, in honor of his 70th birthday, Julian Hawthorne said that he liked Whitman best for the fact that his friendship and personal love of Mr. Lincoln. Mr. Hawthorne had been misinformed. Mr. Whitman never talked to Mr. Lincoln in his life, nor Mr. Lincoln to him.

Whitman did not interrupt banquet speakers and tell them that they were in error as to their facts, still, it is not known that he ever claimed any degree of intimacy with Lincoln.

What did Whitman think of Lincoln while Lincoln was living? Unfortunately, we have little dated material for an answer. In his letter to his mother, June 30, 1863, he says:

Mr. Lincoln passes here (14th street) every evening on the way out. I noticed him about half past 6—he was in

his barouche, two horses, guarded by about thirty
cavalry. The barouche comes first under a slow trot,
driven by one man on the box, not servant or footman
beside: the cavalry all follow closely after with a
lieutenant at their head. I had a good view of the President last evening. He looks more careworn even than
usual, his face cut with deep lines, seams, and his complexion gray through very dark skin—a curious looking
man, very sad. I said to a lady who was looking with
me, "Who can see that man without losing all wish to be
sharp upon him personally?" The lady assented, though
she is almost vindictive on the course of the administration (thinks it wants nerve, etc.,—the usual complaint.)[5]

In this instance he stood up for the President,
but his words can not be called very enthusiastic
praise. On October 27, 1863, he wrote to his
mother:

I have finally made up my mind that Mr. Lincoln has
done as good as a big human man can do. I still think
him a pretty big President.[6]

So far as we know, Whitman printed no single
line in praise while Lincoln was living, and wrote
no testimony of any sort of his affection for the
great President. While Lincoln lived, Whitman
apparently felt some measure of restraint, such as
was common at the time.

We shall do well to remember now and then the
mighty reaction against Lincoln in the elections of
1862, and the heavy vote for the opposition
candidate in 1864. Whitman believed in Lincoln,
and went home to vote for him and to do some work

at the polls; but his enthusiasm was not then such as it became after Lincoln was dead.

While he lived, Whitman guardedly conceded that Lincoln was "a pretty big President"; after Lincoln was dead, he seemed to Whitman "the grandest figure yet on all the crowded canvas of the Nineteenth Century."

Said Walt Whitman concerning Lincoln:

Lincoln is particularly my man—particularly belongs to me; yes, and by the same token, I am Lincoln's man: I guess I particularly belong to him; we are afloat on the same stream—we are rooted in the same ground."

It was an arrogant affirmation, for Whitman was arrogant; so far that matter was Lincoln. Not many men would have had courage to say, "Lincoln is my man." Not many men who might have said it would have been permitted to say it without rebuke. It would not have troubled Whitman if he had been rebuked for saying it, he would have said it all the same; but so far as we know, no one rebuked him, and that is the strange thing about it.

Literary and historical critics have come with rather remarkable unanimity to a large measure of agreement with Whitman's declaration that Lincoln belonged to him. Not simply in his native boastfulness and affirmation of appreciation but by an undeniable kinship of spirit, each of them belonged to the other, and both belonged to America.

XIV

WALT WHITMAN's poems that were to appear under the general title *Drum-Taps,* were largely in manuscript when he first went to Washington in December, 1862. Concerning this manuscript he wrote to his mother when he had decided to remain at the capital, admonishing her to take care of this precious package. He continued to write and revise, and as soon as he had secured his clerkship, and in consequence the money to enable him to go forward, he left his desk and returned to Brooklyn to arrange for the publication of this book at his own expense. It was in course of printing when Lincoln was shot, and there was no poem in the book that made reference to the President. The volume appeared early in 1866. Before many copies had been sold, he issued a pamphlet which was inserted in the remaining copies, that is to say in nearly all of the first edition, which by that insertion became the second. This was entitled *Sequel to Drum-Taps* and professed to be poems written since the preceding came from the press. Most of them were commonplace. That which distinguished the enlarged volume, and did more than any other one thing to insure the fame of Walt Whitman as a poet, was a group of four poems on the death of President Lincoln.

The third, and next to the shortest of these poems, written for the day of Lincoln's burial, was entitled *Hush'd be the Camps To-day,* and the other, a simple quatrain, bore as its title its first line, *This Dust Was Once the Man.* Neither of these would have attracted much attention at the time or have added anything later to the poet's reputation. They may be briefly disposed of here:

HUSH'D BE THE CAMPS TO-DAY
(May 4, 1865)

Hush'd be the camps to-day,
And, soldiers, let us drape our war-worn weapons,
And each with musing soul retire to celebrate,
Our dear commander's death.

No more for him life's stormy conflicts,
Nor victory, nor defeat—no more time's dark events,
Charging like ceaseless.clouds across the sky.
But sing, poet, in our name,
Sing of the love we bore him—because you, dweller in
      camps, know it truly.

As they invault the coffin there,
Sing—as they close the doors of earth upon him—one
      verse,
For the heavy hearts of soldiers.

THIS DUST WAS ONCE THE MAN

This dust was once the man,
Gentle, plain, just and resolute, under whose cautious
    hand,
Against the foulest crime in history known in any land or
    age,
Was saved the Union of these States.

After the publication of the supplement to
Drum-Taps, Whitman wrote no poetry on Lincoln
worth the mention. A few months before his
death, he wrote a short poem for Lincoln's birthday, and it was published February 12, 1888, and
is in the completed edition of *Leaves of Grass.* It
contains two lines only, and is notable only as being
Whitman's last poem on Lincoln.

ABRAHAM LINCOLN, Born Feb. 12, 1809*

To-day, from each and all, a breath of prayer—a pulse
    of thought,
To memory of Him—To birth of Him.

One of these poems on the death of Lincoln was
destined to become Whitman's most famous
literary composition. He did not give it the place
of honor in his *Sequel;* that was reserved, and
rightly, for the longest poem of the group. But it
rose to a height of popularity which no other poem
of Whitman ever attained. In its form it is a

Sands at Seventy, in *Leaves of Grass,* p. 388.
Published Feb. 12, 1888.

denial of every theory of Whitman's concerning poetry. Its four stanzas have eight lines each, four of them long and four short. They have not only meter but rhyme. The poem is the least like Whitman of anything Whitman ever wrote; yet it is his highest literary monument:

O CAPTAIN! MY CAPTAIN!

O Captain! my Captain! our fearful trip is done,
The ship has weather'd every rack, the prize we sought is
    won,
The port is near, the bells I hear, the people all exulting,
While follow eyes the steady keel, the vessel grim and
    daring;
        But O heart! heart! heart!
         O the bleeding drops of red,
           Where on the deck my Captain lies,
           Fallen cold and dead.

O Captain! my Captain! rise up and hear the bells;
Rise up—for you the flag is flung—for you the bugle
    trills,
For you bouquets and ribbon'd wreaths—for you the
    shores a-crowding,
For you they call, the swaying mass, their eager faces
    turning;
        Here, Captain! dear father!
         This arm beneath your head!
          It is some dream that on the deck,
           You've fallen cold and dead.

My Captain does not answer, his lips are pale and still,
My father does not feel my arm, he has no pulse nor will,

The ship is anchor'd safe and sound, its voyage closed
    and done,
From fearful trip the victor ship comes in with object
    won;
      Exult O shores, and ring, O bells!
      But I with mournful tread,
        Walk the deck my Captain lies,
        Fallen cold and dead.

Not the most popular, certainly, but incomparably the noblest of these poems, and the greatest that Whitman ever wrote, is that which he justly placed at the front of his *Sequel*. Walt has told us of his being at home when the news of Lincoln's death arrived, and of the effect of the news upon himself and his mother:

Mother prepared breakfast—and other meals afterward—as usual; but not a mouthful was eaten all day by either of us. We each drank half a cup of coffee; that was all. Little was said. We got every newspaper morning and evening, and the frequent extras of that period, and pass'd them silently to each other. . . .

I remember where I was stopping at the time the season being advanced, there were many lilacs in full bloom. By one of those caprices that enter and give tinge to events without being at all a part of them, I find myself always reminded of the great tragedy of that day by the sight and odor of these blossoms. It never fails.

Lilacs he loved. A single shade-tree stood in front of his bare house in Camden, and in the back yard was a lilac bush. He did not forget the association. The lilacs that suggested the poem, however, were in and near Brooklyn.

President Lincoln's Burial Hymn was what he first intended to call it; but it is vastly better that it should be known by its first line, and that was the title he gave it when first it appeared in print, early in 1866.

Never was there another funeral procession just like that of Abraham Lincoln, as his body was carried from the capital of the nation, by day and by night, through Philadelphia, New York, Albany, Cleveland and other cities to Chicago and thence to his old home at Springfield. And nowhere is there another so noble a description of it as in Walt Whitman's hymn. To be sure, the poem is much too long, and very unequal in its several parts, but the useless are readily eliminated, or may recede into the background of the mind. The funeral train moves with dignified solemnity through the stanzas, now through the daylight and again through the night, and the lilacs are in blossom:

WHEN LILACS LAST IN THE DOORYARD BLOOM'D

1

When lilacs last in the dooryard bloom'd,
And the great star early droop'd in the western sky in
      the night,
I mourn'd, and yet shall mourn with ever-returning
      spring.

Ever-returning spring, trinity sure to me you bring,
Lilac blooming perennial and drooping star in the west,
And thought of him I love.

2

O powerful western fallen star!
O shades of night—O moody, tearful night!
O great star disappear'd—O the black murk that hides
the star!
O cruel hands that hold me powerless—O helpless soul
of me!
O harsh surrounding cloud that will not free my soul.

3

In the dooryard fronting an old farm-house near the
white-wash'd palings,
Stands the lilac-bush tall-growing with heart-shaped
leaves of rich green,
With many a pointed blossom rising delicate, with the
perfume strong I love,
With every leaf a miracle—and from this bush in the
dooryard,
With delicate-color'd blossoms and heart-shaped leaves
of rich green,
A sprig with its flower I break.

4

In the swamp in secluded recesses,
A shy and hidden bird is warbling a song.

Solitary the thrush,
The hermit withdrawn to himself, avoiding the settlements,
Sings by himself a song.

Song of the bleeding throat,
Death's outlet song of life, (for well dear brother I know,
If thou wast not granted to sing thou would'st surely
    die.)

5

Over the breast of the spring, the land, amid cities,
Amid lanes and through old woods, where lately the
    violets peep'd from the ground, spotting the gray
    debris,
Amid the grass in the fields each side of the lanes, passing
    the endless grass,
Passing the yellow-spear'd wheat, every grain from its
    shroud in the dark-brown fields uprisen,
Passing the apple-tree blows of white and pink in the
    orchards,
Carrying a corpse to where it shall rest in the grave,
Night and day journeys a coffin.

6

Coffin that passes through lanes and streets,
Through day and night with the great cloud darkening
    the land,
With the pomp of the inloop'd flags with the cities draped
    in black,
With the show of the States themselves as of crape-veil'd
    women standing,
With processions long and winding and the flambeaus of
    the night,
With the countless torches lit, with the silent sea of faces
    and the unbared heads,
With the waiting depot, the arriving coffin, and the
    sombre faces,

With dirges through the night, with the thousand voices
      rising strong and solemn,
With all the mournful voices; of the dirges pour'd around
      the coffin,
The dim-lit churches and the shuddering organs—where
      amid these you journey,
With the tolling tolling bells' perpetual clang,
Here, coffin that slowly passes,
I give you my sprig of lilac.

7

(Nor for you, for one alone,
Blossoms and branches green to coffins all I bring,
For fresh as the morning, thus would I chant a song for
      you O sane and sacred death.

All over bouquets of roses,
O death, I cover you over with roses and early lilies,
But mostly and now the lilac that blooms the first,
Copious I break, I break the sprigs from the bushes,
With loaded arms I come, pouring for you,
For you and the coffins all of you O death.)

8

O western orb sailing the heaven,
Now I know what you must have meant as a month since
      I walk'd,
As I walk'd in silence the transparent shadowy night,
As I saw you had something to tell as you bent to me
      night after night,
As you droop'd from the sky low down as if to my side,
      (while the other stars all look'd on,)

As we wander'd together the solemn night, (for something
  I know not what kept me from sleep,)
As the night advanced, and I saw on the rim of the west
  how full you were of woe,
As I stood on the rising ground in the breeze in the cool
  transparent night,
As I watch'd where you pass'd and was lost in the
  netherward black of the night,
As my soul in its trouble dissatisfied sank, as where you
  sad orb,
Concluded, dropt in the night, and was gone.

9

Sing on there in the swamp,
O singer bashful and tender, I hear your notes, I hear
  your call,
I hear, I come presently, I understand you,
But a moment I linger, for the lustrous star has detain'd
  me,
The star my departing comrade holds and detains me.

10

O how shall I warble myself for the dead one there I
  loved?
And how shall I deck my song for the large sweet soul
  that has gone?
And what shall my perfume be for the grave of him I
  love?

Sea-winds blown from east and west,
Blown from the Eastern sea and blown from the Western
  sea, till there on the prairies meeting,
These and with these and the breath of my chant,
I'll perfume the grave of him I love.

11

O what shall I hang on the chamber walls?
And what shall the pictures be that I hang on the walls,
To adorn the burial-house of him I love?

Pictures of growing spring and farms and homes,
With the Fourth-month eve at sundown, and the gray
     smoke lucid and bright,
With floods of the yellow gold of the gorgeous, indolent,
     sinking sun, burning, expanding the air,
With the fresh sweet herbage under foot, and the pale
     green leaves of the trees prolific,
In the distance the flowing glaze, the breast of the river,
     with a wind-dapple here and there,
With ranging hills on the banks, with many a line against
     the sky, and shadows,
And the city at hand with dwellings so dense, and stacks
     of chimneys,
And all the scenes of life and the workshops, and the
     workmen homeward returning.

12

Lo, body and soul—this land,
My own Manhattan with spires, and the sparkling and
     hurrying tides, and the ships,
The varied and ample land, the South and the North in
     the light, Ohio's shores and flashing Missouri,
And ever the far-spreading prairies cover'd with grass
     and corn.

Lo, the most excellent sun so calm and haughty,
The violet and purple morn with just-felt breezes,
The gentle soft-born measureless light,

The miracle spreading bathing all, the fulfill'd noon,
The coming eve delicious, the welcome night and the stars,
Over my cities shining all, enveloping man and land.

13

Sing on, sing on you gray-brown bird,
Sing from the swamps, the recesses, pour your chant from
the bushes,
Limitless out of the dusk, out of the cedars and pines.

Sing on dearest brother, warble your reedy song,
Loud human song, with voice of uttermost woe.

O liquid and free and tender!
O wild and loose to my soul—O wondrous singer!
You only I hear—yet the star holds me, (but will soon
depart,)
Yet the lilac with mastering odor holds me.

14

Now while I sat in the day and look'd forth,
In the close of the day with its light and the fields of
spring, and the farmers preparing their crops,
In the large unconscious scenery of my land with its lakes
and forests,
In the heavenly aerial beauty, (after the perturb'd winds
and the storms,)
Under the arching heavens of the afternoon swift passing,
and the voices of children and women,
The many-moving sea-tides, and I saw the ships how they
sail'd,
And the summer approaching with richness, and the fields
all busy with labor,

And the infinite separate houses, how they all went on,
     each with its meals and minutia of daily usages,
And the streets how their throbbings throbb'd, and the
     cities pent—lo, then and there,
Falling upon them all and among them all, enveloping me
     with the rest,
Appear'd the cloud, appear'd the long black trail,
And I knew death, its thought, and the sacred knowledge
     of death.

Then with the knowledge of death as walking one side
     of me,
And the thought of death close-walking the other side
     of me,
And I in the middle as with companions, and as holding
     the hands of companions,
I fled forth to the hiding receiving night that talks not,
Down to the shores of the water, the path by the swamp
     in the dimness,
To the solemn shadowy cedars and ghostly pines so still.

And the singer so shy to the rest receiv'd me,
The gray-brown bird I know receiv'd us comrades three,
And he sang the carol of death, and a verse for him I love.

From deep secluded recesses,
From the fragrant cedars and the ghostly pines so still,
Came the carol of the bird.

And the charm of the carol rapt me,
As I held as if by their hands my comrades in the night,
And the voice of my spirit tallied the song of the bird.

Come lovely and soothing death,
Undulate round the world, serenely arriving, arriving,

In the day, in the night, to all, to each,
Sooner or later delicate death.

Prais'd be the fathomless universe,
For life and joy, and for objects and knowledge curious,
And for love, sweet love—but praise! praise! praise!
For the sure-enwinding arms of cool-enfolding death.

Dark mother always gliding near with soft feet,
Have none chanted for thee a chant of fullest welcome?
Then I chant it for thee, I glorify thee above all,
I bring thee a song that when thou must indeed come,
  come unfalteringly.

Approach strong deliveress,
When it is so, when thou hast taken them I joyously sing
  the dead,
Lost in the loving floating ocean of thee,
Laved in the flood of thy bliss O death.

From me to thee glad serenades,
Dances for thee I propose saluting thee, adornments and
  feastings for thee,
And the sights of the open landscape and the high-spread
  sky are fitting,
And life and the fields, and the huge and thoughtful night.

The night in silence under many a star,
The ocean shore and the husky whispering wave whose
  voice I know,
And the soul turning to thee O vast and well-veil'd death,
And the body gratefully nestling close to thee.

Over the tree-tops I float thee a song,
Over the rising and sinking waves, over the myriad fields
  and the prairies wide,

*Over the dense-pack'd cities all and the teeming wharves
        and ways,*
I float this carol with joy, with joy to thee O death.

15

To the tally of my soul,
Loud and strong kept up the gray-brown bird,
With pure deliberate notes spreading filling the **night.**

Loud in the pines and cedars dim,
Clear in the freshness moist and the swamp-perfume,
And I with my comrades there in the night.

While my sight that was bound in my eyes unclosed,
As to long panoramas of visions.

And I saw askant the armies,
I saw as in noiseless dreams hundreds of battle-flags,
Borne through the smoke of the battles and pierc'd with
        missiles I saw them,
And carried hither and yon through the smoke, and torn
        and bloody,
And at last but a few shreds left on the staffs, (and all
        in silence,)
And the staffs all splinter'd and broken.

I saw battle-corpses, myriads of them,
And the white skeletons of young men, I saw them,
I saw the debris and debris of all the slain soldiers of the
        war,
But I saw they were not as was thought,
They themselves were fully at rest, they suffer'd not,
The living remain'd and suffer'd, the mother suffer'd,
And the wife and the child and the musing comrade
        suffer'd,
And the armies that remain'd suffer'd.

16

Passing the visions, passing the night,
Passing, unloosing the hold of my comrades' hands,
Passing the song of the hermit bird and the tallying song
      of my soul,
Victorious song, death's outlet song, yet varying ever-
      altering song,
As low and wailing, yet clear the notes, rising and falling,
      flooding the night,
Sadly sinking and fainting, as warning and warning, and
      yet again bursting with joy,
Covering the earth and filling the spread of the heaven,
As that powerful psalm in the night I heard from recesses,
Passing, I leave thee lilac with heart-shaped leaves,
I leave thee there in the door yard, blooming, returning
      with spring.

I cease from my song for thee,
From my gaze on thee in the west, fronting the west,
      communing with thee,
O comrade lustrous with silver face in the night.

Yet each to keep and all, retrievements out of the night,
The song, the wondrous chant of the gray-brown bird,
And the tallying chant, the echo arous'd in my soul,
With the lustrous and drooping star with the counte-
      nance full of woe,
With the holders holding my hand nearing the call of the
      bird,
Comrades mine and I in the midst, and their memory ever
      to keep, for the dead I loved so well,
For the sweetest, wisest soul of all my days and lands—
      and this for his dear sake,
Lilac and star and bird twined with the chant of my soul,
There in the fragrant pines and the cedars dusk and dim.

XV

WHITMAN'S writings on Lincoln are of four
kinds. The first are his contemporary notes and
communications, edited, as he did edit them, for
later publication, but considered in this volume as
nearly as possible in their original form. The
second is his magazine article in the *North American Review,* which appeared later with the
Reminiscences of other of Lincoln's contemporaries, in the book edited by Allen Thorndike Rice.
The third is his group of Lincoln poems. The
fourth in his *Lecture on the Death of President
Lincoln.* The first three groups have been given
in full in the preceding chapters. It remains for
us to consider what became in some respects Walt
Whitman's most important contribution to an interpretation of Lincoln, and the only important
one, except his magazine article, written after the
publication of the *Sequel* to *Drum-Taps* in 1865-66.

Whitman's early aspirations to be a lecturer
never wholly forsook him. When he was about
thirty years of age, and already gray, he turned in

his political affiliations from the Democratic party, and became a Free-soiler.

"I guess it was about those years," says his brother George, "he had an idea he could lecture. He wrote what mother called barrels of lectures. We did not know what he was writing. He did not seem more abstracted than usual. He would lie abed late, and after getting up would write a few hours if he took the notion—perhaps would go off the rest of the day. We were all at work—all except Walt."[1]

Professor Perry, in his excellent biography, says:

"This project of lecturing was one to which Whitman kept recurring, to the end of his life. It guided at intervals his desultory reading, and seemed to promise an opportunity for that personal impress upon other men which his nature has now begun to crave."[2]

His career as a lecturer began in an address delivered before the Brooklyn Art Union, March 31, 1851. It was printed in the *Brooklyn Daily Advertiser,* for April third. His success does not appear to have been large enough to justify the hope that he had any notable future on the lecture platform. A few sentences from this lecture, however, he preserved in his *Collect.*[3]

In the summer of 1863, he reverted with rather more than his usual occasional longing to the platform. He was in Washington, not very well, disinclined to enter the army, and without steady employment. He wrote to his mother of his ambition to deliver lectures and raise money. He had been securing modest contributions for his hospital work in answer to his newspaper articles, but he thought he could obtain more both for himself and his cause by lecturing. But reflection convinced him that the time was not opportune, and he gave up the idea.[4]

It is not uncommon to see in print statements to the effect that Whitman was present at the theater and saw Lincoln shot.[5] We know that this was not the case. Whitman was not in the theater, and not in Washington, and he did not return immediately to Washington after the death of Lincoln. But he heard the story from eye-witnesses, and his description is so vivid that Whitman must almost have believed that he saw with his own eyes and heard with his own ears the story which he gives in detail. It will be noticed that all his descriptions repeat the rough language of the infuriated soldiers, and show other marks of his having derived portions of the narrative from men who were actually present. One incident, that of the mad wrath of the mob outside, and the difficulty with which the police saved an innocent from hanging, was in his original record, but omitted from the lecture. Like Defoe's *Journal of the Plague Year*, Whitman told the story so vividly as to compel belief that he was relating what he had seen.

Whitman's chief source of information concerning the events in and about Ford's Theater that night was Peter Doyle. Peter Doyle, as reported by Doctor Burke, said:[6]

Walt was not at the theatre the night Lincoln was shot. It was from me he got all that in the book—they are almost my words. I heard that the President and his wife would be present and made up my mind to go. There was a great crowd in the building. I got into the second gallery. There was nothing extraordinary in the performance. I saw everything on the stage and was in a good position to see the President's box. I heard the pistol shot. I had no idea what it was, what it meant, it was sort of muffled. I really knew nothing of what had occurred until Mrs. Lincoln leaned out of the box and cried, "The President is shot." I needn't tell you what I felt then, or saw. It is all put down in Walt's piece—that piece is exactly right. I saw Booth on the cushion of the box, saw him jump over, saw him catch his foot, which turned, saw him fall on the stage. He got up on his feet, cried out something which I could not hear for the hubbub, and disappeared. I suppose I lingered almost the last person. A soldier came into the gallery, saw me still there, called to me: "Get out of here! we're going to burn this damned building down!" I said: "If that is so, I'll get out!"

It would be interesting to know just when Walt first wrote out his account of the assassination of Lincoln. He afterward said that it was "written at the time." But that, in Walt's vocabulary, is a very elastic phrase. It was not written immediately after the event, for Walt was in Brooklyn.

Edward P. Mitchell, in his *Memories of an Editor: Fifty Years of American Journalism*[7] gives some account of his dealings with Whitman, and says:

The poet of the future was already his own press agent. He was accustomed to send to the paper contributions accompanied by reference paragraphs purporting to be written by the editor. The same is entirely in his own handwriting:

"*Abraham Lincoln*. To-day is the anniversary of President Lincoln's birth. If he had lived till now he would have been sixty-six years old. We call attention to the vivid account, given in another column, of the actual scenes of the assassination, written at the time, by Walt Whitman, and now first published."

If Walt had been correct in his arithmetic, this story of the assassination, "written at the time," should have been in the *New York Sun* for February 12, 1875, and there, at my request, the Library of Congress undertook to find it for me. Not discovering it there, and failing also to find it in newspapers for the days immediately preceding or following, they went forward a year, and discovered this first publication of the story, as Walt declared it to be, in the issue of February 12, 1876.

I am carrying this article over into the Appendix,[8] because to print it here and to follow it with its later variations would make dull reading for any but special students, but for these it has a very real interest, and it must be preserved. The important thing to be remembered just now is that as it was first wrought out by Walt into literary form, it was not done with intent to make a lecture of it, but to make a book about Lincoln; and that Walt did not ever accomplish.

If Walt expected that the publication of his article on the Death of Lincoln on Lincoln's birthday in 1876 would bring him encouragement to go forward and complete a book about Abraham Lincoln, he must have been disappointed. As far as we know, he received no such encouragement. The years slipped along, and no great interest was shown in what he still had to say about Lincoln. He needed money, as usual, and his friends learned that it might be a good time to do something for him.

Just before Lincoln's birthday, 1878, two years after his article in the *Sun,* Walt received a letter[9] from John Burroughs proposing a benefit for Walt, the occasion to be a lecture on Lincoln:

> Esopus, N. Y.
> Feb. 3rd, 1878.
>
> Dear Walt:
>
> Gilder suggests that a "benefit" be got up for you in N. Y. and that you be asked to lecture on Lincoln. He thinks it would go with a rush under proper management & that lots of money might be made. The suggestion seems to me timely & just the thing & we will set the ball agoing if you are willing & have or can have the lecture ready. I saw Stedman when I passed through

N. Y. & liked him. I think he would take hold to give the project a lift. Of course Swinton & many others would too. I think in fact we might have a big time & make it pay. Write me how you feel about it, & if you favor it, how soon you could be on hand.

As ever

John Burroughs.

But nothing came of this immediately. Whitman had no material for a lecture appropriate for the birthday of Lincoln. And apparently it did not occur to him at once that he might deliver a lecture on Lincoln's death. The whole matter went over for a year. Then, in 1879, the invitation was made more definite, and Walt, in lack of other available material, worked over the article that had appeared in the *Sun* in 1876, and called that essay a lecture. He would not be able to stand upon his feet for its delivery, but it was arranged that he should sit. And so, many years after his early ambition, Walt Whitman became a lecturer.

This was really Whitman's one lecture. His youthful career as a lecturer was not a brilliant success. His thought of leaving Washington during the war and going upon the lecture platform came to no result. His paralysis prevented his attempting to make that dream come true in the years following his stroke. His hope of a career upon the platform, when he had sufficiently recovered to cherish such a hope, came down to this, an opportunity to deliver, approximately once a year, and usually upon the anniversary of the death of Lincoln, his vivid account of the tragedy.

How often did he deliver the lecture on the Death of Lincoln?

In Binn's *Life of Whitman* it is stated that he gave it thirteen times. I have not been able to discover so large a total, nor have any of the Whitman authorities whom I have consulted. Prof. Bliss Perry and Prof. Emory Holloway agree that this number is too large. With their assistance, and some research of my own, I am able to give the following list, which may or may not be entirely complete, together with the authorities upon whom I rely:

1. The first delivery of Walt Whitman's lecture on the Death of the President was in Steck Hall, Fourteenth Street, New York, April 14, 1879.[10] Whitman was dreaming of making a pilgrimage up and down the land, giving this lecture and reading his poems. He has told us the story of his hope:

What I came to New York for:— To try the experiment of a lecture—to see whether I could stand it, and whether an audience would—was my specific object. Some friends had invited me—it was by no means clear how it would end—I stipulated that they should get only a third rate hall, and not sound the advertising trumpets a bit and so I started. I much wanted something to do for occupation, consistent with my limping and paralyzed state. And now, since it came off, and since neither my hearers nor I myself really collaps'd at

the aforesaid lecture, I intend to go up and down the
land, (in moderation) seeking whom I may devour, with
lectures, and reading of my own poems—short pulls,
however—never exceeding an hour.[11]

It is to be feared that the sale of tickets was not
large, and the audience not greatly enthusiastic, for
the newspaper account, manifestly friendly, is
strikingly barren of all details that could have in-
dicated great demonstration on the part of the
audience. He delivered the lecture from manuscript, and was seated while he read it, his paralysis
making it impossible for him to stand during its
delivery.

Walt made it known that he desired other engagements; but apparently he did not succeed in
making them. The *New York Tribune* printed
this lecture in full, with this prefatory note:[12]

The poet Walt Whitman made his beginning as a
lecturer last night, at Steck Hall, in Fourteenth St. His
subject was the death of President Lincoln. He reads
from notes, sitting in a chair, as he is still much disabled
from paralysis. He desires engagements as a reader of
his own poems and as a lecturer.

It is not surprising that he was not sought out
by lecture committees, and that the friendly interest of the *Tribune* does not appear to have brought
results. A portion of the spring of 1879, following
the lecture, Walt spent in New York, with friends
whose home overlooked Central Park, and he had

the frequent joy of riding up and down on the Fifth Avenue busses. But he was not in demand as a lecturer.

The spring of 1879 passed, and so did the summer, and Whitman's initial lecture engagement remained his only one. In September of that year he made his western journey, going as far as Denver, and viewing something of the country of which he had written much and seen little. Apparently he delivered no lectures on this trip. Not only did he receive no invitations but the tour proved too strenuous for him, and he spent nearly three months recuperating in the home of his brother in St. Louis, returning to Camden in January, 1880.

2. The second delivery of the Lincoln lecture was in Association Hall, Philadelphia, April 15, 1880. Tickets were sold at fifty cents each, and were initialed "W. W." in Whitman's own hand.[13]

In anticipation of this delievry, Whitman revised his lecture somewhat, and prefaced the paragraph which appears at the opening of the address as given in his *Complete Works*. Apparently he did not greatly change it afterward, except for the additional matter which he gave when he delivered it for the final time. Although he had given it in Boston in 1881 before he put it into his *Complete Works,* the text stands with its reference in the first sentence to the fifteenth anniversary:

How often since that dark and dripping Saturday—that chilly April day, now fifteen years bygone, my heart has entertained the dream, the wish, to give of Abraham Lincoln's death, its own special thought and memorial.

This was not precisely his first thought in preparing the lecture. He hoped that it would be a lecture on Lincoln's life and work, and would make a somewhat popular appeal, but this hope failed, and he reshaped it somewhat into a memorial of Lincoln's death, and the changes made for the second delivery, he did not modify; even the number of the anniversary remained unchanged in the manuscript, and was probably altered orally in the delivery.[14]

3. The third occasion of the delivery of the lecture, was on April 15, 1881,[15] in the Hawthorne Rooms, before The St. Botolph Club of Boston. The lecture itself does not appear to have created large enthusiasm, but the appearance of Whitman in Boston became the occasion of a marked ovation, and had an important relation to the publication of a new edition of his writings.

Whitman has left us a record of this visit to Boston. He found the trip unexpectedly comfortable. "Seems as if all the ways and means of American travel to-day had been settled, not only with reference to speed and directness, but for the comfort of women, children, invalids, and old fellows like me."

He traveled to Boston on the Federal Express,

which had been put on for the Centennial in Philadelphia in 1876, and has now been maintained for
half a century.   Walt tells about the journey in
interesting detail:

I went on by a through train that runs daily from
Washington to the Yankee Metropolis without change.
You get in a sleeping-car, soon after dark in Philadelphia
and after ruminating an hour or two, have your bed made
up if you like, draw the curtains, and go to sleep in it, fly
on through Jersey to New York—hear in your half-
slumbers a dull, jolting sound or two—are unconsciously
toted from Jersey City by a midnight steamer around the
Battery and under the big bridge to the track of the New
Haven road—resume your flight eastward, and early the
next morning you wake up in Boston.

The midnight jolting and ferry transportation
have now been eliminated by the erection of the
Hellgate Bridge, but those features of the journey
are remembered by all the older travelers on this
train.

At the station in Boston he met a stranger who
assisted him through the crowd, ordered a hack and
paid for it, and sent Walt to his hotel, the Revere
House.   Everything was propitious; every one was
kind.

The occasion of my jaunt, I suppose I had better say
here, was for a public reading of "the Death of Abraham
Lincoln" on the sixteenth anniversary of that tragedy;
which reading duly came off, night of April 15.   Then I
linger'd a week in Boston—felt pretty well (the mood

propitious, my paralysis lull'd)—went around everywhere, and saw all that was to be seen, especially human
beings.

He called on Longfellow, and had "a short and
pleasant visit." Whitman said he was not one of
the calling kind, but as Longfellow had called on
him once in Camden, he felt it not only a pleasure
but a duty to return the call. "He was the only
particular eminence I called on in Boston."

All in all, this Boston trip and lecture appear to
have given Whitman a good many happy memories.

Sylvester Baxter, in an article in the *New
England Magazine,* related his account of this visit
of Whitman to Boston in April, 1881, on which
occasion Baxter met Walt for the first time. He
speaks of Whitman as having been invited to "read
his paper on Lincoln"—"a sort of memorial service
which the poet has made it a point to observe somewhere every year on the anniversary of the death of
the great President, whom Whitman honored as
the most representative of the Americans, an incarnation of the spirit of modern democracy."
Baxter was sent by the *Boston Herald* to write an
article on Whitman, and in that way began a last-
ing friendship. Whitman was in the Revere
House, surrounded by a small group of friends,
one of the chief among whom was Truman H.
Bartlett, the sculptor. Whitman sat in an armchair, his big stick in hand. John T. Trowbridge

and Frank B. Sanborn were among his callers. Baxter did not speak of Whitman's address as a lecture, but as a "reading." He said it was "a sort of drawing-room occasion, in the pleasant Hawthorne rooms on Park Street, before a representative and distinguished audience."

Walt said of this visit, "It was well I got away in fine order, for if I had staid another week, I should have been killed with kindness, and with eating and drinking."

He enjoyed Boston, and was surprised to find there as much enterprise and prosperity as he had seen anywhere in the West. In his audience he greatly admired the "fine-looking gray-hair'd women" who comprised so large a fraction of his hearers. They seemed to him "healthy and wifely and motherly and wonderfully charming and beautiful, I think such as no time or land but ours could show."

This visit became the occasion of his tribute to four American poets, in which he did much to remove the impression of contempt and hostility toward his predecessors and contemporaries which some of his earlier writings had produced. The occasion of his writing this tribute was a visit to Longfellow, made on the day following Whitman's lecture. His own record appears in *Specimen Days*:

MY TRIBUTE TO FOUR POETS

April 16. [*1881.*] A short but pleasant visit to Longfellow. I am not one of the calling kind, but as the author
of "Evangeline" kindly took the trouble to come and see
me three years ago in Camden, where I was ill, I felt not
only the impulse of my own pleasure on that occasion,
but a duty. He was the only particular eminence I called
on in Boston, and I shall not soon forget his lit-up face
and glowing warmth and courtesy, in the modes of what
is called the old school.

And now just here I feel the impulse to interpolate
something about the mighty four who stamp this first
American century with its birthmarks of poetic literature.
In a late magazine one of my reviewers, who ought to
know better, speaks of my "attitude of contempt and
scorn and intolerance" toward the leading poets—of my
"deriding" them, and preaching their "uselessness." If
anybody cares to know what I think—and have long
thought and avow'd—about them, I am entirely willing
to propound. I can't imagine any better luck befalling
these States for a poetical beginning and initiation than
has come from Emerson, Longfellow, Bryant, and Whittier. Emerson, to me, stands unmistakably at the head,
but for the others I am at a loss where to give any pre-
cedence. Each illustrious, each rounded, each distinctive.
Emerson for his sweet, vital-tasting melody, rhym'd
philosophy, and poems as amber-clear as the honey of the
wild bee he loves to sing. Longfellow for rich color,
graceful forms and incidents—all that makes life beautiful and love refined—competing with the singers of
Europe on their own ground, and, with one exception,
better and finer work than that of any of them. Bryant
pulsing the first interior verse-throbs of a mighty world—
bard of the river and the wood, ever conveying a taste of

open air, with scents as from hayfields, grapes, birch-borders—always lurkingly fond of threnodies—beginning and ending his long career with chants of death, with here and there through all, poems, or passages of poems, touching the highest universal truths, enthusiasms, duties—morals as grim and eternal, if not as stormy and fateful, as anything in Eschylus. While in Whittier, with his special themes—(his outcropping love of heroism and war, for all his Quakerdom, his verses at times like the measur'd step of Cromwell's old veterans)—in Whittier lives the zeal, the moral energy, that founded New England—the splendid rectitude and ardor of Luther, Milton, George Fox—I must not, dare not, say the wilfulness and narrowness—though doubtless the world needs now, and always will need, most above all, just such narrowness and wilfulness.

This visit had an important bearing upon the publication of a new and complete edition of Whitman's poems, by the house of James R. Osgood & Company. This arrangement led to Whitman's return to Boston about the middle of August, in order to see his book through the press. His room was at the Hotel Bulfinch, a rather famous boarding-house near the Revere House. For about two months he was in the city. His own records extend to the middle of October. During this period, President Garfield died, about ten-thirty P. M. September 19, 1881. The analogy to Lincoln's death came strongly to his imagination, and he wrote these lines for the *Boston Sunday Globe:*

THE SOBBING OF THE BELLS

(Midnight, September 19-20, 1881)

The sobbing of the bells, the sudden death-news every-
    where,
The slumberers rouse, the rapport of the People,
(Full well they know that message in the darkness,
Full well return, respond within their breasts, their
    brains, the sad reverberations,)
The passionate toll and clang—city to city, joining,
    sounding, passing,
Those heart-beats of a Nation in the night.

It was a notable coincidence that joined in this
city of Boston the reading of Walt's lecture on the
death of Lincoln with a short, sad interpretation of
the message of the tolling bells that woke the land
at midnight to the sorrowful tidings of the death
by assassination of another President.

This double visit of Whitman's to Boston gave
him a needful contact with the life of other literary
men. Too much had he lived in a critical seclusion
with his hand against the hands of others. This
visit enabled him to make a visit, under the
guidance of Frank B. Sanborn, to Emerson, then
with mind eclipsed but with a gentle smile, and to
recall Emerson's earnest but futile attempt,
twenty-one years previous, to dissuade Walt from
publishing portions of his *Children of Adam.*

A VISIT, AT THE LAST, TO R. W. EMERSON

Concord, Mass.—Out here on a visit—elastic, mellow, Indian-summery weather. Came to-day from Boston, (a pleasant ride of 40 minutes by steam, through Somerville, Belmont, Waltham, Stony Brook, and other lively towns,) convoy'd by my friend F. B. Sanborn, and to his ample house, and the kindness and hospitality of Mrs. S. and their fine family. Am writing this under the shade of some old hickories and elms, just after 4 P. M., on the porch, within a stone's throw of the Concord river. Off against me, across stream, on a meadow and side-hill, hay-makers are gathering and wagoning-in probably their second or third crop. The spread of emerald-green and brown, the knolls, the score or two of little haycocks dot-ting the meadow, the loaded-up wagons, the patient horses, the slow-strong action of the men and pitchforks— all in the just-waning afternoon, with patches of yellow sun-sheen, mottled by long shadows—a cricket shrilly chirping, herald of the dusk—a boat with two figures noiselessly gliding along the little river, passing under the stone bridge-arch—the slight settling haze of aerial moisture, the sky and the peacefulness expanding in all directions and overhead—fill and soothe me.

Same Evening.—Never had I a better piece of luck befall me: a long and blessed evening with Emerson, in a way I couldn't have wish'd better or different. For nearly two hours he has been placidly sitting where I could see his face in the best light, near me. Mrs. S.'s back-parlor well fill'd with people, neighbors, many fresh and charming faces, women, mostly young, but some old. My friend A. B. Alcott and his daughter Louisa were there early. A good deal of talk, the subject Henry Thoreau—some new glints of his life and fortunes, with letters to and from him—one of the best by Margaret

Fuller, others by Horace Greeley, Channing, &c.—one
from Thoreau himself, most quaint and interesting. (No
doubt I seem'd very stupid to the roomful of company,
taking hardly any part in the conversation; but I had
"my own pail to milk in," as the Swiss proverb puts it.)
My seat and the relative arrangement were such that,
without being rude, or anything of the kind, I could just
look squarely at E., which I did a good part of the two
hours. On entering, he had spoken very briefly and
politely to several of the company, then settled himself
in his chair, a trifle push'd back, and, though a listener
and apparently an alert one, remain'd silent through the
whole talk and discussion. A lady quietly took a seat
next him, to give special attention. A good color in his
face, eyes clear, with the well-known expression of sweet-
ness, and the old clear-peering aspect quite the same.

Next Day.—Several hours at E.'s house, and dinner
there. An old familiar house, (he has been in it thirty-
five years,) with surroundings, furnishment, roominess,
and plain elegance and fullness, signifying democratic
ease, sufficient opulence, and an admirable old-fashioned
simplicity—modern luxury, with its mere sumptuousness
and affectation, either touch'd lightly upon or ignored
altogether. Dinner the same. Of course the best of the
occasion (Sunday, September 18, '81) was the sight of
E. himself. As just said, a healthy color in the cheeks,
and good light in the eyes, cheery expression, and just the
amount of talking that best suited, namely, a word or
short phrase only where needed, and almost always with
a smile. Besides Emerson himself, Mrs. E., with their
daughter Ellen, the son Edward and his wife, with my
friend F. S. and Mrs. S., and others, relatives and inti-
mates. Mrs. Emerson, resuming the subject of the evening before, (I sat next to her,) gave me further and
fuller information about Thoreau, who, years ago, during

Mr. E.'s absence in Europe, had lived for some time in the family, by invitation.

OTHER CONCORD NOTATIONS

Though the evening at Mr. and Mrs. Sanborn's, and the memorable family dinner at Mr. and Mrs. Emerson's, have most pleasantly and permanently fill'd my memory, I must not slight other notations of Concord. I went to the old Manse, walk'd through the ancient garden, enter'd the rooms, noted the quaintness, the unkempt grass and bushes, the little panes in the windows, the low ceilings, the spicy smell, the creepers embowering the light. Went to the Concord battle ground, which is close by, scann'd French's statue, "the Minute Man," read Emerson's poetic inscription on the base, linger'd a long while on the bridge, and stopp'd by the grave of the unnamed British soldiers buried there the day after the fight in April, '75. Then riding on, (thanks to my friend Miss M. and her spirited white ponies, she driving them,) a half hour at Hawthorne's and Thoreau's graves. I got out and went up of course on foot, and stood a long while and ponder'd. They lie close together in a pleasant wooded spot well up the cemetery hill, "Sleepy Hollow." The flat surface of the first was densely cover'd by myrtle, with a border of arbor-vitæ, and the other had a brown headstone, moderately elaborate, with inscriptions. By Henry's side lies his brother John, of whom much was expected, but he died young. Then to Walden pond, that beautiful embower'd sheet of water, and spent over an hour there. On the spot in the woods where Thoreau had his solitary house is now quite a cairn of stones, to mark the place; I too carried one and deposited on the heap. As we drove back, saw the "School of Philosophy," but it was shut up, and I would not have it open'd for me.

Near by stopp'd at the house of W. T. Harris, the Hegelian, who came out, and we had a pleasant chat while I sat in the wagon. I shall not soon forget those Concord drives, and especially that charming Sunday forenoon one with my friend Miss M., and the white ponies.

BOSTON COMMON—MORE OF EMERSON

Oct. 10-13.—I spend a good deal of time on the Common, these delicious days and nights—every mid-day from 11.30 to about 1—and almost every sunset another hour. I know all the big trees, especially the old elms along Tremont and Beacon streets, and have come to a sociable-silent understanding with most of them, in the sunlit air, (yet crispy-cool enough,) as I saunter along the wide un-paved walks. Up and down this breadth by Beacon street, between these same old elms, I walk'd for two hours, of a bright sharp February mid-day twenty-one years ago, with Emerson, then in his prime, keen, physically and morally magnetic, arm'd at every point, and when he chose, wielding the emotional just as well as the intellectual. During those two hours he was the talker and I the listener. It was an argument-statement, reconnoitring, review, attack, and pressing home, (like an army corps in order, artillery, cavalry, infantry,) of all that could be said against that part (and a main part) in the construction of my poems, "Children of Adam." More precious than gold to me that dissertion—it afforded me, ever after, this strange and paradoxical lesson; each point of E.'s statement was unanswerable, no judge's charge ever more complete or convincing, I could never hear the points better put—and then I felt down in my soul the clear unmistakable conviction to disobey all, and pursue my own way. "What have you to say then to such things?" said E., pausing in conclusion. "Only that

while I can't answer them at all, I feel more settled than
ever to adhere to my own theory, and exemplify it," was
my candid response.   Whereupon we went and had a
good dinner at the American House.   And thenceforward
I never waver'd or was touch'd with qualms, (as I confess
I had been two or three times before).

4. The fourth delivery of the lecture was in
Camden, at Morton Hall, March 1, 1886. If there
were intervening lectures, I have found no record
of them.   The trouble concerning the publication
of his Boston edition occurred in 1882, and it is not
certain that he was invited to lecture in that or the
years immediately following.

5. The fifth lecture of which I have discovered
a record, was in Philadelphia, at the Chestnut
Street Opera House, April 15, 1886.[16]

The immediate result of this lecture was the
bringing to Whitman of six hundred dollars, and
for that purpose, the lecture was arranged.   Whitman felt so happy about the result, he presented
each of the attendants at the theater two dollars.
That, for Walt, was extravagant generosity.

6. The next occasion on which we are certain
that Whitman delivered this lecture, was in Unity
Church, Camden, on April 6, 1887.   Of this event,
we have very little record.   Kennedy says:

On April 6, 1887, Whitman read his Lincoln at the
Unitarian Church in Camden, "holding the rapt attention
of the large audience for an hour."[17]

We have an echo of this occasion in a conversation which occurred in Whitman's home several months later. Under date of Friday, October 5, 1888, Traubel writes of one of the several visits of James Hunter to Whitman:

When he got to talking about Hunter, he warmed up right away. "He came in, was chatty; I enjoyed him. . . . I guess you know Hunter was a rebel—hot, hot: what they called dyed in the wool, sees everything through that one glass, colored by it, nothing at all coming to him from any other source. That question of the War is the only one over which we threatened to come to words. I know I roused up once or twice when we got on that subject: I have tried to keep shy of it; but Hunter himself is a challenge—he won't let you avoid it. I told W. that Hunter resented his reference to Lincoln's death as a 'murder.' H. had heard W. read the lecture at Unity Church."[18]

7. The seventh time this lecture was delivered, was in New York, at the Madison Square Theater, April 15, 1887.[19]

This was the most brilliant of the occasions on which Whitman gave this address, and also the most profitable financially. Andrew Carnegie sent his check for three hundred and fifty dollars for a box, which, however, he does appear to have occupied. Other and equally distinguished people were present, including Samuel L. Clemens, Moncure D. Conway, Frank Stockton, Edward Eggleston, James Russell Lowell, Richard Watson Gilder, Augustus St. Gaudens, John Burroughs and other literary men. That evening Whitman was given a reception at the Westminster Hotel. He was in high spirits over the event.

The preparations for the lecture in Madison Square Theater appear to have been much more elaborate than those of any previous delivery. Richard Watson Gilder borrowed from the *Century* the excellent little line cut of Hesler's portrait of Lincoln then in use by that magazine, and secured Major Pond as manager. The tickets of admission were large and contained full information. This little cut of Lincoln adorned the upper left-hand corner and the ticket read:

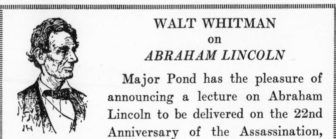

WALT WHITMAN
on
ABRAHAM LINCOLN

Major Pond has the pleasure of announcing a lecture on Abraham Lincoln to be delivered on the 22nd Anniversary of the Assassination, Thursday, April 14th, at 4 o'clock P. M., in the

MADISON SQUARE THEATER
NEW YORK

Reserved Seats $1.50, Admission $1.00. Tickets for sale at the Theater. Orders may be sent to Maj. J. B. Pond, Everett House; E. C. Stedman, 66 Broadway-44 E. 26 St.; J. H. Johnston, Lotus Club; R. W. Gilder, 33 E. 17th St.: Brentano's, Union Square.

Concerning this delivery, we have more than our usual rather meager information. Largely the people who bought tickets were those who honored Whitman and wished to assist him. There was not a very large audience. Even though high prices were paid for the boxes, there appears to have been plenty of seats. A very thin volume by Stuart Merrill, issued in Toronto in 1922, gives that author's recollections of this lecture, as delivered in Madison Square Theater:

I met Walt Whitman in New York, four or five years before his death. He had come, according to his touching custom, on the day of the anniversary of Abraham Lincoln's assassination, to deliver a lecture on the great president. . . . I will never forget our long wait in the huge cold theater, dimly lighted, musty smelling, a thinly scattered audience of devotees whose whispering made audible the silence inside and the deafening hubbub without. . . .

Walt Whitman! Here he is, half paralyzed, hardly able to walk, leaning with his right hand on a cane, and heavily with his left on that of the poet Stedman. With the aid of his friend he was installed in a great armchair, before papers which he hardly touched, allowing himself to slowly improvise. And how affecting this was! He related the death of Abraham Lincoln quite simply, as though the event had taken place the evening before. Not a gestulation, no raising of the voice. I was there; everything happened to me. His address was as gripping as the reports of the tragedies of Eschylus. Nothing has proved to me more plainly the fact that eloquence consists only of emotion and sincerity of the orator.

At the end of the lecture, some one asked that Walt Whitman should recite "O Captain! My Captain!" the ode dedicated by him to the memory of Lincoln. The poor voice of the old man exerted itself anew, a little before sunset, sobbing, rather than chanting the funeral verses. . . . The voice died away in the noise of the applause, which appeared to me an outrage to the grief of the poet.

J. H. Johnston, a jeweler, who was one of the prime movers in arranging for the Madison Square Theater address, wrote a glowing account of it afterward:

Early in March, 1887, I telephoned Edmund Clarence Stedman, asking him to meet me at the office of Richard Watson Gilder, editor of the *Century* magazine. I also telephoned Major J. B. Pond, the lecture agent. When we met, I reminded them that the 15th of April would be the twenty-second anniversary of the death of Abraham Lincoln, and would it not be a good idea to bring Walt Whitman over from Camden on that date and have him deliver his lecture on the Death of Lincoln in some Theater and give him the cash results? They all exclaimed, "Capital!" and I said, "If you will back me up with your assistance, I will go ahead and manage it. I have already secured the Madison Square Theater for the afternoon of that day." Then Mr. Stedman said, "Say, fellows, if it should happen to be a stormy day and a small audience, and a loss was made, it wouldn't be fair to let Johnston shoulder the loss. So let us four agree that if there is a loss we will divide it among us four." To which they all agreed.

The day came, a perfect charming day, and the house was packed. James Russell Lowell occupied a box with friends. At the close of the reading, the little six-year old daughter of Mr. Gilder walked from the wings to the center of the stage, and handing Walt a bouquet, exclaimed, "Here are some lilacs that in our garden bloomed!" The house went wild with applause, Walt taking her up in his arms and kissing her. And just at that moment, I reached Mr. Lowell's box, and introduced myself. Wiping the tears from his eyes, he said to me, "Mr. Johnston, this has been one of the most impressive hours of my life."

Mr. Gilder wrote me two days before the reading, "Dear Mr. Johnston, General Sherman is in town; wouldn't it be a fine thing to offer him and his family a box for Walt's reading?" I answered, "By all means." And so the great General was with us.

Walt stayed all night at the Westminster Hotel, occupying the same suite of rooms that Charles Dickens did while in New York, and during the evening, over two hundred callers came and paid homage to the "Good Grey Poet." Walt afterward told me that it was the culminating hour of his life.[20]

8. The eighth occasion on which Whitman appears to have delivered this address was in New York on April 14, 1889. He did not lecture on the anniversary of Lincoln's death in 1888, possibly because he was not very well, but more likely because no invitation came to him. Traubel records long conversations on the fourteenth and fifteenth of April, 1888, Whitman being engaged in sorting

and burning up old manuscripts.   Traubel records
no lecture either in 1888 or 1889, though his published volumes do not cover the anniversary of
Lincoln's death in the latter year.   The biographers
seem to think Whitman too ill to have lectured in
either year.   But we have one witness to his delivery of the address in New York in 1889.   John
Hay, who was in New York, having a good-
natured quarrel with Gilder because the *Century*
was cutting chapters of the *Life of Lincoln* then
appearing in that magazine, wrote to Nicolay,
April 15, 1889:

Whitman's lecture yesterday was quite interesting as
to audience and accessories.   The lecture itself is about
all in print, nothing whatever new.[21]

9. The ninth delivery of the lecture, if our count
is complete, was in Philadelphia, on April 15, 1890.
Kennedy has this account of it:[22]

Thursday night, April 15, 1890, Whitman rose from
a sick bed, crying, "Dangers retreat when boldly they're
confronted," and went over, hoarse and half blind, to
read his "Death of Lincoln" lecture before a gay and
crowded audience at the Art Club Rooms, 220 South
Broad Street, Philadelphia, under the auspices of the
Contemporary Club.   He had to be helped and led every
step, but his intellectual force, it was noted, was not in
the least abated.

This was Whitman's last lecture, and the *Boston*

Transcript's correspondent said it was the thirteenth time he had delivered it. Whitman himself said he had given it ten or twelve times. He was not very accurate in his count of such matters.[23]

Of this last delivery, the *Transcript's* correspondent said:

The most of the poet's address was devoted to the actual occurrences and details of the murder. We believe the delivery Tuesday was Whitman's thirteenth of it. The old poet is now physically wrecked. But his voice and magnetism are the same. For the last month he has been suffering under a severe attack of the prevailing influenza, the grip, in accumulation upon his previous ailments, and above all, that terrible paralysis, the bequest of secession war times. He was dressed last Tuesday night in an entire suit of French Canadian grey wool cloth, with broad shirt collar, with no necktie; long white hair, red face, full beard and moustache, and looked as though he might weigh two hundred pounds. He had to be helped and led every step. In five weeks more he will begin his seventy-second year. He is still writing a little. He crawled out of his sick-bed and went over, hoarse and half blind, to deliver his memorable essay on the death of Lincoln, on the twenty-fifth anniversary of the tragedy.

On this last delivery of the lecture, Whitman prefaced a new paragraph, which is given in the Appendix to this volume.[24]

On October 21, 1890, Whitman made his last public appearance, as the guest of honor at a lecture delivered for his benefit by Robert G.

Ingersoll, at Horticultural Hall, in Philadelphia.
Whitman was wheeled on the stage in an invalid's
chair, and at the close of Ingersoll's address he
spoke a few words of thanks to the audience. After
that, the years of invalidism were succeeded by a
swifter downward tendency. Pneumonia developed, and he recovered only partly from its
effects. He died March 26, 1892.

This, then, is Walt Whitman's final attempt to
interpret Abraham Lincoln to his own generation
and to the generation that had grown up since
Lincoln's death. It began in a description of the
death of the great President, and it wrought out
more fully than its first intent promised an estimate
of Lincoln's life and influence. Except for the
prefatory remarks at the time of its last delivery,
he did not modify it after its delivery in Boston in
1881. The following is the form in which is left
to posterity Walt Whitman's tribute to the
memory of Abraham Lincoln:

DEATH OF ABRAHAM LINCOLN

LECTURE *deliver'd in New York, April 14, 1879—in
Philadelphia, '80—in Boston, '81.*

How often since that dark and dripping Saturday—
that chilly April day, now fifteen years bygone—my
heart has entertain'd the dream, the wish, to give of
Abraham Lincoln's death, its own special thought and
memorial. Yet now the sought-for opportunity offers, I

find my notes incompetent, (why, for truly profound themes, is statement so idle? why does the right phrase never offer?) and the fit tribute I dream'd of, waits unprepared as ever. My talk here indeed is less because of itself or anything in it, and nearly altogether because I feel a desire, apart from any talk, to specify the day, the martyrdom. It is for this, my friends, I have call'd you together. Oft as the rolling years bring back this hour, let it again, however briefly, be dwelt upon. For my own part, I hope and desire, till my own dying day, whenever the 14th or 15th of April comes, to annually gather a few friends, and hold its tragic reminiscence. No narrow or sectional reminiscence. It belongs to these States in their entirety—not the North only, but the South—perhaps belongs most tenderly and devoutly to the South, of all; for there, really, this man's birthstock. There and thence his antecedent stamp. Why should I not say that thence his manliest traits—his universality—his canny, easy ways and words upon the surface—his inflexible determination and courage at heart? Have you never realized it, my friends, that Lincoln, though grafted on the West, is essentially, in personnel and character, a Southern contribution?

And though by no means proposing to resume the secession war tonight, I would briefly remind you of the public conditions preceding that contest. For twenty years, and especially during the four or five before the war actually began, the aspect of affairs in the United States, though without the flash of military excitement, presents more than the survey of a battle, or any extended campaign, or series, even of Nature's convulsions. The hot passions of the South—the strange mixture at the North of inertia, incredulity, and conscious power—the incendiarism of the abolitionists—the rascality and *grip* of the politicians, unparallel'd in any land, any age.

To these I must not omit adding the honesty of the
essential bulk of the people everywhere—yet with all the
seething fury and contradiction of their natures more
arous'd than the Atlantic's waves in wildest equinox. In
politics, what can be more ominous, (though generally
unappreciated then)—what more significant than the
Presidentiads of Fillmore and Buchanan? proving conclusively that the weakness and wickedness of elected
rulers are just as likely to afflict us here, as in the
countries of the Old World, under their monarchies,
emperors, and aristocracies. In that Old World were
everywhere heard underground rumblings, that died out,
only to again surely return. While in America the
volcano, though civic yet, continued to grow more and
more convulsive—more and more stormy and threatening.

In the height of all this excitement and chaos, hovering
on the edge at first, and then merged in its very midst,
and destined to play a leading part, appears a strange
and awkward figure. I shall not easily forget the first
time I ever saw Abraham Lincoln. It must have been
about the 18th or 19th of February, 1861. It was rather
a pleasant afternoon, in New York city, as he arrived
there from the West, to remain a few hours, and then
pass on to Washington, to prepare for his inauguration.
I saw him in Broadway, near the site of the present Post-
office. He came down, I think from Canal street, to stop
at the Astor House. The broad spaces, sidewalks, and
street in the neighborhood, and for some distance, were
crowded with solid masses of people, many thousands.
The omnibuses and other vehicles had all been turn'd off,
leaving an unusual hush in that busy part of the city.
Presently two or three shabby hack barouches made their
way with some difficulty through the crowd, and drew up
at the Astor House entrance. A tall figure stepp'd out
of the centre of these barouches, paus'd leisurely on the

sidewalk, look'd up at the granite walls and looming
architecture of the grand old hotel—then, after a relieving stretch of arms and legs, turn'd round for over a
minute to slowly and good-humoredly scan the appearance of the vast and silent crowds. There were no
speeches—no compliments—no welcome—as far as I
could hear, not a word said. Still much anxiety was
conceal'd in that quiet. Cautious persons had fear'd some
mark'd insult or indignity to the President-elect—for he
possess'd no personal popularity at all in New York city,
and very little political. But it was evidently tacitly
agreed that if the few political supporters of Mr. Lincoln
present would entirely abstain from any demonstration
on their side, the immense majority, who were anything
but supporters, would abstain on their side also. The
result was a sulky, unbroken silence, such as certainly
never before characterized so great a New York crowd.

Almost in the same neighborhood I distinctly remember'd seeing Lafayette on his visit to America in 1825.
I had also personally seen and heard, various years
afterward, how Andrew Jackson, Clay, Webster, Hungarian Kossuth, Filibuster Walker, the Prince of Wales
on his visit, and other celebres, native and foreign, had
been welcom'd there—all that indescribable human roar
and magnetism, unlike any other sound in the universe—
the glad exulting thunder-shouts of countless unloos'd
throats of men! But on this occasion, not a voice—not
a sound. From the top of an omnibus, (driven up one
side, close by, and block'd by the curbstone and the
crowds,) I had, I say, a capital view of it all, and especially of Mr. Lincoln, his look and gait—his perfect composure and coolness—his unusual and uncouth height, his
dress of complete black, stovepipe hat push'd back on the
head, dark-brown complexion, seam'd and wrinkled yet
canny-looking face, black, bushy head of hair, dispropor-

tionately long neck, and his hands held behind as he stood observing the people. He look'd with curiosity upon that immense sea of faces, and the sea of faces return'd the look with similar curiosity. In both there was a dash of comedy, almost farce, such as Shakspere puts in his blackest tragedies. The crowd that hemm'd around consisted I should think of thirty to forty thousand men, not a single one his personal friend—while I have no doubt, (so frenzied were the ferments of the time,) many an assassin's knife and pistol lurk'd in hip or breast-pocket there, ready, soon as break and riot came.

But no break or riot came. The tall figure gave another relieving stretch or two of arms and legs; then with moderate pace, and accompanied by a few unknown-looking persons, ascended the portico-steps of the Astor House, disappear'd through its broad entrance—and the dumb-show ended.

I saw Abraham Lincoln often the four years following that date. He changed rapidly and much during his Presidency—but this scene, and him in it, are indelibly stamp'd upon my recollection. As I sat on the top of my omnibus, and had a good view of him, the thought, dim and inchoate then, has since come out clear enough, that four sorts of genius, four mighty and primal hands, will be needed to the complete limning of this man's future portrait—the eyes and brains and finger-touch of Plutarch and Eschylus and Michel Angelo, assisted by Rabelais.

And now—(Mr. Lincoln passing on from this scene to Washington, where he was inaugurated, amid armed cavalry, and sharp-shooters at every point—the first instance of the kind in our history—and I hope it will be the last)—now the rapid succession of well-known events, (too well known—I believe, these days, we almost hate to hear them mention'd)—the national flag fired on at

Lincoln's First Portrait, 1848   Lincoln in 1858

Lincoln in 1863   Lincoln's Last Photograph

Sumter—the uprising of the North, in paroxysms of
astonishment and rage—the chaos of divided councils—
the call for troops—the first Bull Run—the stunning
cast-down, shock, and dismay of the North—and so in full
flood the secession war. Four years of lurid, bleeding,
murky, murderous war. Who paint those years, with all
their scenes?—the hard-fought engagements—the defeats, plans, failures—the gloomy hours, days, when our
Nationality seem'd hung in pall of doubt, perhaps
death—the Mephistophelean sneers of foreign lands and
attachés—the dreaded Scylla of European interference,
and the Charybdis of the tremendously dangerous latent
strata of secession sympathizers throughout the free
States, (far more numerous than is supposed)—the long
marches in summer—the hot sweat, and many a sunstroke, as on the rush to Gettysburg in '63—the night
battles in the woods, as under Hooker at Chancellorsville—the camps in winter—the military prisons—the
hospitals—(alas! alas! the hospitals.)

The secession war? Nay, let me call it the Union war.
Though whatever call'd, it is even yet too near us—too
vast and too closely overshadowing—its branches unform'd yet, (but certain,) shooting too far into the
future—and the most indicative and mightiest of them
yet ungrown. A great literature will yet arise out of the
era of those four years, those scenes—era compressing
centuries of native passion, first-class pictures, tempests
of life and death—an inexhaustible mine for the histories,
drama, romance, and even philosophy, of peoples to
come—indeed the verteber of poetry and art, (of personal
character too,) for all future America—far more grand,
in my opinion, to the hands capable of it, than Homer's
siege of Troy, or the French wars to Shakspere.

But I must leave these speculations, and come to the
theme I have assign'd and limited myself to. Of the

actual murder of President Lincoln, though so much has been written, probably the facts are yet very indefinite in most persons' minds. I read from my memoranda, written at the time, and revised frequently and finally since.

The day, April 14, 1865, seems to have been a pleasant one throughout the whole land—the moral atmosphere pleasant too—the long storm, so dark, so fratricidal, full of blood and doubt and gloom, over and ended at last by the sun-rise of such an absolute National victory, and utter break-down of Secessionism—we almost doubted our own senses! Lee had capitulated beneath the apple-tree of Appomattox. The other armies, the flanges of the revolt, swiftly follow'd. And could it really be, then? Out of all the affairs of this world of woe and failure and disorder, was there really come the confirm'd, unerring sign of plan, like a shaft of pure light—of rightful rule—of God? So the day, as I say, was propitious. Early herbage, early flowers, were out. (I remember where I was stopping at the time, the season being advanced, there were many lilacs in full bloom. By one of those caprices that enter and give tinge to events without being at all a part of them, I find myself always reminded of the great tragedy of that day by sight and odor of these blossoms. It never fails.)

But I must not dwell on accessories. The deed hastens. The popular afternoon paper of Washington, the little "Evening Star," has spatter'd all over its third page, divided among the advertisements in a sensational manner, in a hundred different places, *The President and his Lady will be at the Theatre this evening.* . . . (Lincoln was fond of the theatre. I have myself seen him there several times. I remember thinking how funny it was that he, in some respects the leading actor in the stormiest drama known to real history's stage through centuries, should sit there and be so completely interested and absorb'd in those human jack-straws, moving about with their silly little gestures, foreign spirit, and flatulent text.)

On this occasion the theatre was crowded, many ladies in rich and gay costumes, officers in their uniforms, many well-known citizens, young folks, the usual clusters of gas-lights, the usual magnetism of so many people, cheerful, with perfumes, music of violins and flutes—(and over all, and saturating all, that vast, vague wonder, *Victory*, the nation's victory, the triumph of the Union, filling the air, the thought, the sense, with exhilaration more than all music and perfumes.)

The President came betimes, and, with his wife, wit-ness'd the play from the large stage-boxes of the second tier, two thrown into one, and profusely drap'd with the national flag. The acts and scenes of the piece—one of those singularly written compositions which have at least the merit of giving entire relief to an audience engaged in mental action or business excitements and cares during the day, as it makes not the slightest call on either the moral, emotional, esthetic, or spiritual nature—a piece, ("Our American Cousin,") in which, among other char-acters, so call'd, a Yankee, certainly such a one as was never seen, or the least like it ever seen, in North America, is introduced in England, with a varied fol-de-rol of talk, plot, scenery, and such phantasmagoria as goes to make up a modern popular drama—had progress'd through perhaps a couple of its acts, when in the midst of this comedy, or non-such, or whatever it is to be call'd, and to offset it, or finish it out, as if in Nature's and the great Muse's mockery of those poor mimes, came interpolated that scene, not really or exactly to be described at all, (for on the many hundreds who were there it seems to this hour to have left a passing blur, a dream, a blotch)—and yet partially to be described as I now proceed to give it. There is a scene in the play representing a modern parlor,

in which two unprecedented English ladies are inform'd
by the impossible Yankee that he is not a man of fortune,
and therefore undesirable for marriage-catching purposes; after which, the comments being finish'd, the
dramatic trio make exit, leaving the stage clear for a
moment. At this period came the murder of Abraham
Lincoln. Great as all its manifold train, circling round
it, and stretching into the future for many a century, in
the politics, history, art, &c., of the New World, in point
of fact the main thing, the actual murder, transpired with
the quiet and simplicity of any commonest occurrence—
the bursting of a bud or pod in the growth of vegetation,
for instance. Through the general hum following the
stage pause, with the change of positions, came the muffled
sound of a pistol-shot, which not one-hundredth part of
the audience heard at the time—and yet a moment's
hush—somehow, surely, a vague startled thrill—and
then, through the ornamented, draperied, starr'd and
striped space-way of the President's box, a sudden figure,
a man, raises himself with hands and feet, stands a
moment on the railing, leaps below to the stage, (a
distance of perhaps fourteen or fifteen feet,) falls out of
position, catching his boot-heel in the copious drapery,
(the American flag,) falls on one knee, quickly recovers
himself, rises as if nothing had happen'd, (he really
sprains his ankle, but unfelt then)—and so the figure,
Booth, the murderer, dress'd in plain black broadcloth,
bare-headed, with full, glossy, raven hair, and his eyes like
some mad animal's flashing with light and resolution, yet
with a certain strange calmness, holds aloft in one hand
a large knife—walks along not much back from the footlights—turns fully toward the audience his face of
statuesque beauty, lit by those basilisk eyes, flashing with
desperation, perhaps insanity—launches out in a firm and
steady voice the words *Sic semper tyrannis*—and then

walks with neither slow nor very rapid pace diagonally across to the back of the stage, and disappears. (Had not all this terrible scene—making the mimic ones preposterous—had it not all been rehears'd, in blank, by Booth, beforehand?)

A moment's hush—a scream—the cry of *murder*—Mrs. Lincoln leaning out of the box, with ashy cheeks and lips, with involuntary cry, pointing to the retreating figure, *He has kill'd the President*. And still a moment's strange, incredulous suspense—and then the deluge!—then that mixture of horror, noises, uncertainty—(the sound, somewhere back, of a horse's hoofs clattering with speed)—the people burst through chairs and railings, and break them up—there is inextricable confusion and terror—women faint—quite feeble persons fall, and are trampl'd on—many cries of agony are heard—the broad stage suddenly fills to suffocation with a dense and motley crowd, like some horrible carnival—the audience rush generally upon it, at least the strong men do—the actors and actresses are all there in their play-costumes and painted faces, with mortal fright showing through the rouge—the screams and calls, confused talk—redoubled, trebled—two or three manage to pass up water from the stage to the President's box—others try to clamber up—&c., &c.

In the midst of all this, the soldiers of the President's guard, with others, suddenly drawn to the scene, burst in—(some two hundred altogether)—they storm the house, through all the tiers, especially the upper ones, inflam'd with fury, literally charging the audience with fix'd bayonets, muskets and pistols, shouting *Clear out! clear out! you sons of*——. . . . . Such the wild scene, or a suggestion of it rather, inside the play-house that night.

Outside, too, in the atmosphere of shock and craze, crowds of people, fill'd with frenzy, ready to seize any outlet for it, come near committing murder several times on innocent individuals. One such case was especially exciting. The infuriated crowd, through some chance, got started against one man, either for words he utter'd, or perhaps without any cause at all, and were proceeding at once to actually hang him on a neighboring lamp-post, when he was rescued by a few heroic policemen, who placed him in their midst, and fought their way slowly and amid great peril toward the station house. It was a fitting episode of the whole affair. The crowd rushing and eddying to and fro—the night, the yells, the pale faces, many frighten'd people trying in vain to extricate themselves—the attack'd man, not yet freed from the jaws of death, looking like a corpse—the silent, resolute, half-dozen policemen, with no weapons but their little clubs, yet stern and steady through all those eddying swarms—made a fitting side-scene to the grand tragedy of the murder. They gain'd the station house with the protected man, whom they placed in security for the night, and discharged him in the morning.

And in the midst of that pandemonium, infuriated soldiers, the audience and the crowd, the stage, and all its actors and actresses, its paint-pots, spangles, and gaslights—the life blood from those veins, the best and sweetest of the land, drips slowly down, and death's ooze already begins its little bubbles on the lips.

Thus the visible incidents and surroundings of Abraham Lincoln's murder, as they really occur'd. Thus ended the attempted secession of these States; thus the four years' war. But the main things come subtly and invisibly afterward—neither military, political, nor (great as those are,) historical. I say, certain secondary and indirect results, out of the tragedy of this death, are, in my opinion, greatest. Not the event of the murder itself. Not that Mr. Lincoln strings the principal points and personages of the period, like beads, upon the single string of his career. Not that his idiosyncrasy, in its sudden appearance and disappearance, stamps this Republic with a stamp more mark'd and enduring than any yet given by any one man—(more even than Washington's;)—but, join'd with these, the immeasurable value and meaning of that whole tragedy lies, to me, in senses finally dearest to a nation, (and here all our own)—the imaginative and artistic senses—the literary and dramatic ones. Not in any common or low meaning of those terms, but a meaning precious to the race, and to every age. A long and varied series of contradictory events arrives at last at its highest poetic, single, central, pictorial denouement. The whole involved, baffling, multiform whirl of the secession period comes to a head, and is gather'd in one brief flash of lightning-illumination—one simple, fierce deed. Its sharp culmination, and as it were solution, of so many bloody and angry problems, illustrates those climax-moments on the stage of universal Time, where the historic Muse at one entrance, and the tragic Muse at the other, suddenly ringing down the curtain, close an immense act in the long drama of creative thought, and give it radiation, tableau, stranger than fiction. Fit radiation—fit close! How the imagination—how the student loves these things! America, too, is to have them. For not in all great deaths, nor far or near—not Cæsar in the roman senate-house, or Napoleon passing away in the wild night-storm at St. Helena—not Paleologus, falling, desperately fighting, piled over dozens deep with Grecian corpses—not calm old Socrates, drinking the hemlock—outvies that terminus of the secession war, in one man's life, here in our midst, in our own time— that seal of the emancipation of three million slaves—that parturition and delivery of our at last really free Republic, born again, henceforth to commence its career of genuine homogeneous Union, compact, consistent with itself.

Nor will ever future American Patriots and Unionists, indifferently over the whole land, or North or South, find a better moral to their lesson. The final use of the greatest men of a Nation is, after all, not with reference to their deeds in themselves, or their direct bearing on their times or lands. The final use of a heroic-eminent life—especially of a heroic-eminent death—is its indirect filtering into the nation and the race, and to give, often at many removes, but unerringly, age after age, color and fibre to the personalism of the youth and maturity of that age, and of mankind. Then there is a cement to the whole people, subtler, more underlying, than any thing in written constitution, or courts or armies—namely, the cement of a death identified thoroughly with that people, at its head, and for its sake. Strange, (is it not?) that battles, martyrs, agonies, blood, even assassination, should so condense—perhaps only really, lastingly condense—a Nationality.

I repeat it—the grand deaths of the race—the dramatic deaths of every nationality—are its most important inheritance-value—in some respects beyond its literature and art—(as the hero is beyond his finest portrait, and the battle itself beyond its choicest song or epic.) Is not here indeed the point underlying all tragedy? the famous pieces of the Grecian masters—and all masters? Why, if the old Greeks had had this man, what trilogies of plays—what epics—would have been made out of him! How the rhapsodies would have recited him! How quickly that quaint tall form would have enter'd into the region where men vitalize gods, and gods divinify men! But Lincoln, his times, his death—great as any, any age—belong altogether to our own, and our autochthonic. (Sometimes indeed I think our American days, our own stage—the actors we know and have shaken hands, or talk'd with—more fateful than any thing in Eschylus—more heroic than the fighters around Troy—afford kings of men for our Democracy prouder than Agamemnon—models of character cute and hardy as Ulysses—deaths more pitiful than Priam's.)

When, centuries hence, (as it must, in my opinion, be centuries hence before the life of these States, or of Democracy, can be really written and illustrated,) the leading historians and dramatists seek for some personage, some special event, incisive enough to mark with deepest cut, and mnemonize, this turbulent Nineteenth century of ours, (not only these States, but all over the political and social world)—something, perhaps, to close that gorgeous procession of European feudalism, with all its pomp and caste-prejudices, (of whose long train we in America are yet so inextricably heirs)—something to identify with terrible identification, by far the greatest revolutionary step in the history of the United States, (perhaps the greatest of the world, our century)—the absolute extirpation and erasure of slavery from the States—those historians will seek in vain for any point to serve more thoroughly their purpose, than Abraham Lincoln's death.

Dear to the Muse—thrice dear to Nationality—to the whole human race—precious to this Union—precious to Democracy—unspeakably and forever precious—their first great Martyr Chief.

NOTES AND COMMENTS

NOTES AND COMMENTS

CHAPTER I

[1]For the biographical information when there is no point at issue, I depend mainly on the biographies of Whitman by Prof. Bliss Perry and Prof. Emory Holloway. I have consulted practically if not quite all the *Lives* of Whitman in the English language, but most of them, however entertaining and however suggestive in the matter of literary criticism, show little evidence of authentic research. In a few places my own studies do not lead me to the same conclusions with Professors Holloway and Perry, but in the main I find them accurate. As what I am here undertaking is not a biography either of Lincoln or of Whitman, I do not find it necessary to overload this section with needless references. The two volumes above referred to are the ones that I mainly rely upon for biographical data, and I am personally indebted to both authors for further assistance.

[2]*In Re Walt Whitman*, p. 35.

[3]The poems quoted in this chapter are from *Drum-Taps*, published in 1866, and conveniently available in Holloway's *Leaves of Grass*, Inclusive Edition.

[4]*A History of the United States during Lincoln's Administration*, by John Bach McMaster, pp. 225-227.

[5]*The Life of Abraham Lincoln*, by William E. Barton, Vol. II, pp. 155-157.

CHAPTER II

[1]*Battles and Leaders of the Civil War*, Vol. III., various chapters.

[2]*The History of the United States during Lincoln's Administration*, by John Bach McMaster, pp. 194 *seq.*

[3]Barton's *Lincoln*, Vol. II., pp. 150 *seq.*

CHAPTER III

[1]Walt Whitman's note-books for the period of the war are in the Manuscripts Division of the Library of Congress, where I have personally examined them. In this visit to the army he did not sleep in his brother's tent, but in that of Captain Sims of Brooklyn.

[2]This quotation also I copy from Walt's pocket note-book.

[3]Professor Holloway especially has sought to prove all things and hold fast that which is true, but even he has been misled occasionally. Professor Perry's biography deals more with the literary than the personal element, and does not profess the same extent of original research.

[4]*The Uncollected Poetry and Prose of Walt Whitman*, Edited by Emory Holloway. Vol. II, p. 21. Professor Holloway accepts this letter as a veracious statement of Walt's activities at Falmouth, but he has not compared it as carefully as I with the manuscripts in the Library of Congress.

[5]Subsequently, in an account professedly written at the time and on the spot, Walt thus told the story of his Falmouth experiences and his introduction to hospital service in Washington:

"Falmouth, Va., opposite Fredericksburgh, December 21, 1862. "Begin my visits among the camp hospitals in the army of the Potomac. Spend a good part of the day in a large brick mansion on the banks of the Rappahannock, used as a hospital since the battle—seems to have receiv'd only the worst cases. Outdoors, at the foot of a tree, within ten yards of the front of the house, I notice a heap of amputated feet, legs, arms, hands, etc., a full load for a one-horse cart. Several dead bodies lie near, each cover'd with its brown woolen blanket. In the dooryard, towards the river, are fresh graves, mostly of officers, their names on pieces of barrel-staves or broken boards, stuck in the dirt. (Most of these bodies were subsequently taken up and transported north to their friends.) The large mansion is quite crowded upstairs and down, everything impromptu, no system, all bad enough, but I have no doubt the best that can be done; all the wounds pretty bad, some frightful, the men in their old clothes, unclean and bloody. Some of the wounded are rebel soldiers and officers, prisoners. One, a Mississippian, a captain, hit badly in leg, I talk'd with some time; he ask'd me for papers, which I gave him (I saw him three months afterward in Washington, with his leg amputated, doing well). I went through the rooms, downstairs and up. Some of the men were dying. I had nothing to give at that visit, but wrote a few letters to folks home, mothers, etc. Also talk'd to three or four, who seem'd most susceptible to it, and needing it."

"December 23 to 31.

"The results of the late battle are exhibited everywhere about here in thousands of cases (hundreds die every day), in the camp, brigade and division hospitals. These are merely tents, and sometimes very poor ones, the wounded lying on the ground, lucky if their blankets are spread on layers of pine or hemlock twigs, or small leaves. No cots; seldom a mattress. It is pretty cold. The ground is frozen hard, and there is occasional snow. I go around from one case to another. I do not see that I do much good to these wounded and dying; but I can not leave them. Once in a while some youngster holds on to me convulsively, and I do what I can for him; at any rate, stop with him and sit near him for hours, if he wishes it.

"Besides the hospitals, I also go occasionally on long tours through the camps, talking with the men, etc. Sometimes at night among the groups around the fires, in their shebang enclosures of bushes. These are curious shows, full of characters and groups. I soon get acquainted anywhere in camp, with officers or men, and am always well used. Sometimes I go down on picket with the regiments I know best. As to rations, the army here at present seems to be tolerably well supplied, and the men have enough, such as it is, mainly salt pork and hard tack. Most of the regiments lodge in the flimsy little shelter-tents. A few have built themselves huts of logs and mud, with fireplaces."

"January, '63.

"Left camp at Falmouth, with some wounded, a few days since, and came here by Aquia Creek railroad, and so on government steamer up the Potomac. Many wounded were with us on the cars and boat. The cars were just common platform ones. The railroad journey of ten or twelve miles was made mostly before sunrise. The soldiers guarding the road came out from their tents or shebangs of bushes with rumpled hair and half-awake look. Those on duty were walking their posts, some on banks over us, others down far below the level of the track. I saw large cavalry camps off the road. At Aquia Creek landing were numbers of wounded going north. While I waited some three hours, I went around among them. Several wanted word sent home to parents, brothers, wives, etc., which I did for them (by mail the next day from Washington). On the boat I had my hands full. One poor fellow died going up.

"I am now remaining in and around Washington, daily visiting the hospitals. Am much in Patent Office, Eighth Street, H. Street, Armory Square, and others. Am now able to do a little good, having money (as almoner of other's home), and getting experience. To-day, Sunday afternoon and till nine in the evening, visited Campbell hospital; attended specially to one case in ward I, very sick with pleurisy and typhoid fever, young man, farmer's son, D. F. Russell, Company E, 60th New York, down-hearted and feeble; a long time before he would take any interest; wrote a letter home to his mother, in Malone, Franklin County, N. Y., at his request; gave him some fruit and one or two other gifts; envelopes and directed his letter, etc. Then went thoroughly through Ward 6, observ'd every case in the ward, without, I think, missing one; gave perhaps from twenty to thirty persons, each one some little gift, such as oranges, apples, sweet crackers, figs, etc."

"Thursday, Jan 21.

"Devoted the main part of the day to Armory Square Hospital; went pretty thoroughly through Wards F, G, H and I; some fifty cases in each ward. In Ward F supplied the men throughout with writing paper and stamp'd envelope each; distributed in small portions, to proper subjects, a large jar of first-rate preserv'd berries, which had been donated to me by a lady—her own cooking. Found several cases I thought good subjects for small sums of money, which I furnish'd. (The wounded men often come up broke, and it helps their spirits to have even the small sum I give them.) My paper and envelopes all gone, but distributed a good lot of amusing reading matter; also, as I thought judicious, tobacco, oranges, apples, etc. Interesting cases in Ward I; Charles Miller, bed 19, Company D, 53d Pennsylvania, is only 16 years of age, very bright, courageous boy, left leg amputated below the knee; next bed to him, another lad very sick; gave each appropriate gifts. In the bed above, also, amputation of the left leg; gave him a little jar of raspberries; bed 1, this ward, gave a small sum; also to a soldier on crutches, sitting on his bed near. . . . (I am more and more surprised at the very great proportion of youngsters from fifteen to twenty-one in the army. I afterwards found a still greater proportion among the southerners.)

"Evening, same day, went to see D. F. R., before alluded to; found him remarkably changed for the better; up and dress'd—quite a triumph; he afterwards got well, and went back to his regiment. Distributed in the wards a quantity of note-paper, and forty or fifty stamp'd envelopes, of which I had recruited my stock, and the men were much in need."

[6]These two records of weight are so near together in point of time, we may have to allow something for differences in the scales. But both are Walt's own record. He weighed more than was well for him.

CHAPTER IV

[1]This very interesting volume, with Walt's scrawling and unsystematic records, is in the Library of Congress.

[2]The first and, as I judge, the most important of his articles appeared in the *New York Times*, February 16, 1863, and in the *Brooklyn Eagle* for March nineteenth.

[3]Walt's book *The Wound-Dresser* is worth reading.

[4]These are Walt's two passes, and so far as we know they are the only ones he ever had during the war. He

was accustomed to save such things. Neither of these was issued by high authority or implied any unusual prerogative. Neither of them passed him outside the lines: The words in italics are those in writing:

HEADQUARTERS MILITARY DISTRICT
WASHINGTON, D. C., *March 25, 1864.*

No. *238*   Not transferrable.

Pass the Bearer *Walter Whitman* within the limits of the Fortifications to *Arlington* and return. This pass will expire on *return trip.*

By order of John H. Martendale
Brig. Gen. and Military Governor
A. S. Gumee, Capt. Ast. Adj. Gen.

HEADQUARTERS MILITARY DISTRICT
WASHINGTON, D. C., *May 14, 1864.*

No. *133.*   Not transferrable.

Pass the bearer *W. Whitman* within the limits of the Fortifications to *Alexandria* and return.

Reason *Business.*

This pass will expire *May 31, 1864.*

By order of
M. N. Wisewel
Col. and Military Guard
W. H. Rogers
Capt. and A. A. S. C.

On the reverse of each is the oath of allegiance and the following description:

Age *45.*

Height *6 ft.*   Hair *Grey*

Complexion *Ruddy.*   Eyes *Blue*

CHAPTER V

[1]John Burroughs' estimate of Walt Whitman is now definitely known to have been written by Whitman himself. Burroughs went quite as far as an honest man ought, both in 1867 and in the nineties in permitting Walt to celebrate himself over John Burroughs' name.

[2]The *Calamus* correspondence I have never been able to read with any degree of satisfaction, but there are those who like it.

CHAPTER VI

[1]From Whitman's *Memoranda of the War*.

[2]The same.

[3]Walt Whitman's diary for 1864, October 31. Library of Congress.

[4]*Reminiscences of Abraham Lincoln by Distinguished Men of His Time*, Edited by Allen Thorndike Rice.

[5]This address is given in Nicolay's *Works of Abraham Lincoln*, Volume XI, pp. 55-56, and in Lapsley's *Works of Lincoln*, Volume VII, pp. 336-338. The best contemporary account of the event was in the *New York Times*, and is preserved in Raymond's *Life of Lincoln*.

CHAPTER VII

[1]In the material which Mr. Rankin furnished for *Who's Who* he claimed to have been a student in Lincoln's office from December, 1856, until February, 1861. He was born April 7, 1837, and died in Springfield, August 15, 1927. His first book, based on his alleged intimacy with Lincoln and Herndon as a student in their office was published in 1916, after Lincoln had been dead fifty-one years and Herndon and his more intimate associates had long been dead. Honorable Newton Bateman was

Superintendent of Public Instruction. His office was not in the same building with the office of Lincoln and Herndon.

CHAPTER VIII

[1]O'Connor's tract has become a very scarce item. The title is, *The Good Gray Poet: a Vindication.* By William Douglas O'Connor. Published by Bruce and Huntington, 458 Broome Street, 1866. It is dated, September 2, 1865.

[2]*With Walt Whitman at Camden,* Sunday, November 25, 1888. Volume III, pp. 177-180.

[3]The text of the letter as here printed is from the original, owned by Mr. Oscar Lion of New York, by whose kind permission I have examined the original. He has added to my obligation by causing a photostatic copy to be made for my use.

[4]I am indebted to various members of the old Van Rensselaer family for very complete information as to the family as it existed in Civil War days.

CHAPTER IX

[1]For details in this chapter see McMasters' *History of the United States during Lincoln's Administration,* and Barton's *Lincoln.*

CHAPTER X

[1]Whitman's Story of the appointment of Harlan is in all editions of Whitman's prose works.

[2]The story of Whitman's dismissal bulks large in all biographies of the poet. As I am about to give Harlan's own account of the matter, and that for the first time, so far as I know, in any work on Whitman, it may be

well to give what I regard as the best connected account
of this affair, from Walt's point of view, that given by
his friend Dr. R. M. Bucke, who, of course, derived his
information from Walt:

"Some time after the close of the War, he (Walt) was
appointed to a clerkship in the Department of the
Interior, but was shortly afterwards discharged by a new
Secretary, Hon James Harlan, 'because he was the author
of an indecent book.' He was immediately given an
equally good place (secured through the good offices of
W. D. O'Connor and J. Hubley Ashton) in the office of
Attorney General James Speed. The dismissal brought
out the pamphlet called *The Good Gray Poet*, which was
adjudged at the time by Henry J. Raymond to be the
most brilliant monogram in American Literature. It is
worth while to put on record here a brief memorandum
of the dismissal. Walt Whitman at the period was divid-
ing all his spare time between visits to the wounded and
sick still left in the several army hospitals in Washington,
and composing the poem, *When Lilacs Last in the Dooryard Bloom'd*. The morning after he was dismissed, his
friend, Mr. Ashton (who had himself sat in the President's
Cabinet, and who occupied a national legal position)
drove down to the Patent Office and had a long interview
with Secretary Harlan on the subject of the dismissal.
The Assistant Secretary of the Interior, Judge Otto, was
present, but took no part in the discourse. Mr. Ashton
asked why Whitman was dismissed, whether he had been
inattentive to his duties or incompetent for them. Mr.
Harlan said, No, there was no complaint on those points;
so far, as he knew, Whitman was a competent and faithful
clerk. Mr. Ashton said, 'Then what is the reason?' Mr.
Harlan answered, 'Whitman is the author of *Leaves of
Grass*.' Mr. Ashton said, 'Is *that* the reason?' The
Secretary said, 'Yes, it is'—and then made a statement

essentially to the following purport: He was exploring the Department after office hours, and in one of the rooms he found *Leaves of Grass*. He took it up and thought it so odd that he carried it to his office a while then examined it. There were marks by or upon the pieces all through the book. He found in some of these marked passages matter so outrageous that he determined to discharge the writer."

The narrative proceeded to state that Ashton told Harlan in detail about Whitman's life and service in the hospitals, and that Harlan said this information modified his opinion concerning the man, but not concerning the book. So the dismissal stood. This was Bucke's rendering of the incident as he gave it eighteen years after in 1883.

³Walt left among his papers a contemporary memorandum in his own hand-writing. It is written on the stationery of the Attorney-General's office and dated Washington, September 26, 1865.

"The acting Secretary of the Interior, Wm. T. Otto, on his way to Cabinet meeting, called at the Att. Gen's Office, on business, and stopt at my desk a moment. He said, 'I hope you are well situated here—I was sorry to lose your services in our Department for I considered them valuable.' The affair (my dismissal) was settled upon before I knew of it.

"In the course of the conversation then and there the question was asked Mr. Otto of the particular copy of *Leaves of Grass* which Mr. Harlan had had in his room, as alluded to in his conversation with the Ass't Gen. whether it was a volume bound in blue paper, like this, pointing to a volume of *Leaves*, paper bound, blue octavo, and he said he had no special conference with Mr. Harlan on the volume (a 500 page paper bound volume like on the table that was shown him). He said it was such a

volume he had seen on Mr. Harlan's desk, a volume of
Leaves of Grass, in blue paper wrappers and the pages
of the poems were marked more or less all through the
book, he remembers the volume was shown him and opened
by some one who saw on his, Mr. O's table, a copy of
Drum-Taps."

'Mr. O'Connor was not unaware that he shared with
Walt the glory of the pamphlet, *The Good Gray Poet.*
That tract brought him a degree of recognition which he
would gladly have received again. In 1882 the Osgood firm
in Boston undertook to bring out the complete edition of
Leaves of Grass for which Walt had been long hoping.
Complaint was made to the Boston District Attorney,
and, though the *Boston Herald,* and *Globe* and the
Springfield Republican published editorials advising the
District Attorney to keep his hands off, Mr. Osgood de-
clined to go forward with the publication. He settled
with Walt by paying him one hundred dollars in cash,
and giving him the plates and two hundred and twenty-
five copies in sheets. Rees, Welsh and Company of
Philadelphia took over the book, and, thanks to the
publicity thus received were able to sell out the entire
edition. Welsh tried hard to get the Philadelphia Society
for the Suppression of Vice to forbid its publication,
doing a good deal of underground work to secure this
result, but without success. But it was the free advertising of the book at this time, and not any general interest
in the work itself, that gained for Walt the money with
which to buy his Camden house.

There certainly was no occasion for O'Connor to rush
in. Walt needed opposition more than he needed defense.
But O'Connor's soul was in arms and he was eager for
the fray. On April twenty-eighth he wrote to John
Burroughs:

"I have just been thunderstruck by a letter—telling me

that Osgood, under a threat from the District Attorney—
has stopped the publication of Walt's book. I don't let
the grass grow under my feet when an outrage of this
kind is committed—and I am going to make the District
Attorney regret that he was ever born, if I can compass
it. As soon as I read Bucke's letter I flew down-stairs to
the Solicitor of the Treasury—I gave the District Attorney unlimited volcano. I am next going straight to the
Attorney General, taking, if possible, Bob Ingersoll along
with me. If we don't raise the biggest row ever dreamed
of, I'm mistaken.

"Osgood—the infernal idiot—should have defied the
District Attorney, published his official warning as an
advertisement, stood a suit, won it, and sold a million
copies of Walt's book on the strength of it. The jackass!

"Excuse the scrawl. I am trembling with fury, and
with the fervor of my oration downstairs."

O'Connor took a month to look up his historical and
literary references, and then wrote his furious phillipic
which appeared in the *New York Tribune* under date of
May 25, 1882. He said in his eloquent peroration:

"On such a subject no thinking man or woman in such
a country as ours will reflect with cold composure. The
action of this lawyer [District Attorney] constitutes a
reef which threatens with shipwreck every great book of
every great author, from Aristophanes to Moliere, from
Æschylus to Victor Hugo; and the drop of blood that is
calm in view of such an outrage proclaims us bastard to
the lineage of the learned and the brave.

"Who knows—but that we may yet, step by step, succeed in bringing the fourteenth century into the nineteenth, and reerect Montfaucon—that hideous edifice of
scaffolds reared by Philippe le Bel, where the blackened
corpse of Glanus swung beside the carcass of the regicide
for having translated Plato, and where Peter Albin

dangled gibbeted beside the robber for having published Virgil?"

But alas, his article evoked no such applause as that which had greeted his *Good Gray Poet*. He was unable to call forth a second peal of thunder like the first. Walt probably was grateful, but he did not need it. O'Connor would have done better if he had joined Welsh and contrived to get the book excluded from the mail.

CHAPTER XI

[1]This letter, notifying Walt of his final discharge, came to my knowledge through Mr. James F. Drake, dealer in Autographs, who informed me that the letter had been sold by him, and who procured a copy through the courtesy of the present owner.

[2]For the description of Walt's home in Mickle Street I am chiefly indebted to Professor Perry.

CHAPTER XII

[1]For data regarding Whitman, see the biographies of Perry and Holloway; for Lincoln, *The Life of Abraham Lincoln*, by William E. Barton.

[2]"In one respect only does Whitman, during these ten years and later, seem to have failed in the finer obligations of friendship. He accepted the worship of these younger men, who gave freely of their time, their literary zeal, their scanty money, in championing his cause. He allowed them to think that in certain aspects of his past experience—challenged by the enemy, and passionately defended by them—his life was known to them. And it was not. Loquacious as was *Leaves of Grass* in the mystical frenzies of the confessionals, the actual Walt

Whitman was shrewdly reticent." Perry, *Life of Whitman*, pp. 212-213.

I agree with the above, except that I am sure this was not the only time Walt failed in fairness to his friends.

CHAPTER XIII

[1]*With Walt Whitman at Camden*, by Horace Traubel.

[2]This is a Brady photograph, in which Lincoln stands with one hand behind his back. In the Meserve Collection, which gives to Lincoln portraits their recognized enumeration, this is Number 56.

[3]*With Walt Whitman at Camden*, May 6, 1888.

[4]*Walt Whitman the Man.*

[5]*Walt Whitman's Memoranda of the War; Written on the Spot in 1863-65.* This little book, now very scarce, was published in 1875. Its contents are available in his *Complete Prose*. His letters to his mother appear to have been edited less than some other parts of the work.

[6]*The Wound-Dresser*, pp. 90, 139.

CHAPTER XIV

[1]The poems in this chapter are from *Drum-Taps*; the Second Edition with the *Sequel;* the narrative portions from Whitman's *Complete Works*.

CHAPTER XV

[1]*In Re Walt Whitman.*

[2]Perry, p. 49.

[3]*Complete Prose Works*, p. 371. See also for additional paragraphs, Perry, p. 49.

[4]The *Wound-Dresser*, pp. 109, 153; Perry, p. 140.

[5]Such an article I saw not long ago in an old copy of *The Truth Seeker*, of New York, along with much else about Walt which appeared to indicate that its search for truth had not been very industrious.

[6]This very interesting interview in *The Complete Works of Walt Whitman*, Putnam edition, Volume IV., pp. 3-16. As Walt had so much to say about Peter, it is interesting to find what Peter had to say about Walt.

[7]These "Memories" after having appeared in the magazine, were published by Scribner's in book form, in 1924.

[8]In the Library of Congress, I found among the Whitman papers, innumerable scraps of the manuscript that gradually evolved into this article, and later into the lecture. I was able to arrange them into some approach to order, and they have now been arranged in this sequence in a scrap-book prepared by the Library. The first bringing into unity of this fragmentary material was not, however, the lecture, but the article which Whitman intended as a chapter in a book he never wrote. This chapter has a special interest, and I give it as it appeared in the *New York Sun*, printed from Walt's own manuscript, on Lincoln's birthday of 1876:

"ABRAHAM LINCOLN'S DEATH

"Walt Whitman's Account of the Scene at Ford's Theatre.

"To-day is the anniversary of President Lincoln's birth. If he had lived till now he would have been sixty-six years old. The following vivid description of the scenes at Ford's Theatre at the time of his assassination, from a forthcoming book by Walt Whitman, has never before been published:

"The day, April 14, 1865, seems to have been a pleasant one throughout the whole land—the moral atmosphere pleasant, too—the long storm, so dark, so fratricidal, full of blood and doubt and gloom, over and ended at last by the sunrise of such an absolute national victory, and utter breaking down of secessionism—we almost doubted our own senses! Lee had capitulated beneath the apple tree of Appomattox. The other armies, the flanges of the revolt, swiftly followed.

"And could it really be, then? Out of all the affairs of this world of woe and passion, of failure and disorder and dismay, was there really come the confirmed, unerring sign of plan, like a shaft of pure light—of rightful rule— of God?

"But I must not dwell on accessories. The deed hastens. The popular afternoon paper, the little *Evening Star*, had spattered all over its third page, divided among the advertisements in a sensational manner in a hundred different places: 'The President and his lady will be at the theatre this evening.' (Lincoln was fond of the theatre. I have myself seen him there several times. I remember thinking how funny it was that he, in some respects, the leading actor in the greatest and stormiest drama known to real history's stage, through centuries, should sit there and be so completely interested and absorbed in those human jackstraws, moving about with their silly little gestures, foreign spirit, and flatulent text.)

"So the day, as I say, was propitious. Early herbage, early flowers, were out. (I remember where I was stopping at the time, the season being advanced, there were many lilacs in full bloom. By one of those caprices that enter and give tinge to events without being at all a part of them, I find myself always reminded of the great tragedy of that day by the sight and odor of these blossoms. It never fails.)

"On this occasion the theatre was crowded, many ladies in rich and gay costumes, officers in their uniforms, many well-known citizens, young folks, the usual clusters of gaslights, the usual magnetism of so many people, cheerful, with perfumes, music of violins and flutes—(and over all, and saturating all, that vast vague wonder, *Victory*, the Nation's Victory, the triumph of the Union, filling the air, the thought, the sense, with exhilaration more than all perfumes.)

"The President came betimes, and, with his wife, witnessed the play, from the large stage boxes of the second tier, two thrown into one, and profusely draped with the national flag. The acts and scenes of the piece—one of those singularly witless compositions which have at least the merit of giving entire relief to an audience engaged in mental action or business excitements and cares during the day, as it makes not the slightest call on either the moral, emotional, esthetic, or spiritual nature—a piece ('Our American Cousin') in which, among other characters, so called, a Yankee, certainly such a one as was never seen, or the least like it ever seen in North America, is introduced in England, with a varied fol-de-dol of talk, plot, scenery, and such phantasmagoria as goes to make up a modern popular drama—had progressed through perhaps a couple of its acts, when in the midst of this comedy, or tragedy, or non-such, or whatever it is to be called, and to off-set it or flush it out, as if in nature's and the great muse's mockery of these poor mimes, comes interpolated that scene, not really or exactly to be described at all (for on the many hundreds who were there it seems to this hour to have left little but a passing blur, a dream, a blotch)—and yet partially to be described as I now proceed to give it.

"There is a scene in the play representing a modern parlor, in which two unprecedented English ladies are in-

formed by the unprecedented and impossible Yankee that
he is not a man of fortune, and therefore undesirable for
marriage catching purposes; after which, the comments
being finished, the dramatic trio make exit, leaving the
stage clear for a moment. There was a pause, a hush as
it were. At this period came the murder of Abraham
Lincoln. Great as that was, with all its manifold train
circling round it, and stretching into the future for many
a century, in the politics, history, art, &c., of the New
World, in point of fact the main thing, the actual murder,
transpired with the quiet and simplicity of any commonest
occurrence—the bursting of a bud or pod in the growth
of vegetation, for instance.

"Through the general hum following the stage pause,
with the change of positions, &c., came the muffled sound
of a pistol shot, which not one hundredth part of the
audience heard at the time—and yet a moment's hush—
somehow, surely a vague, startled thrill—and then,
through the ornamented, draperied, starred and striped
space-way of the President's box, a sudden figure, a man
raises himself with hands and feet, stands a moment on
the railing, leaps below to the stage (a distance of perhaps fourteen or fifteen feet), falls out of position, catching his boot-heel in the copious drapery (the American
flag), falls on one knee, quickly recovers himself, rises as
if nothing had happened (he really sprains his ankle,
but unfelt then)—and so the figure, Booth the murderer,
dressed in plain black broadcloth, bare-headed, with a
full head of glossy, raven hair, and his eyes, like some mad
animal's, flashing with light and resolution, yet with a
certain strange calmness, holds aloft in one hand a large
knife—walks along not much back from the footlights—
turns fully toward the audience his face of statuesque
beauty, lit by those basilisk eyes, flashing with desperation, perhaps insanity—launches out in a firm and steady

voice the words, *Sic semper tyrannis*—and then walks
with neither slow nor very rapid pace diagonally across
to the back of the stage, and disappears. (Had not all
this terrible scene—making the mimic ones preposterous—had it not all been rehearsed, in blank, by Booth,
beforehand?)

"A moment's hush, incredulous—a scream—the cry of
murder—Mrs. Lincoln leaning out of the box, with ashy
cheeks and lips, with involuntary cry, pointing to the
retreating figure, 'He has killed the President.' And still
a moment's strange, incredulous suspense—and then the
deluge!—then that mixture of horror, noises, uncertainty—(the sound, somewhere back, of a horse's hoofs
clattering with speed)—the people burst through chairs
and railings, and break them up—that noise adds to the
queerness of the scene—there is inextricable confusion
and terror—women faint—quite feeble persons fall, and
are trampled on—many cries of agony are heard—the
broad stage suddenly fills to suffocation with a dense
and motley crowd, like some horrible carnival—the
audience rush generally upon it—at least the strong men
do—the actors and actresses are all there in their play
costumes and painted faces, with mortal fright showing
through the rouge, some trembling—some in tears—the
screams and calls, confused talk—redoubled, trebled—two
or three manage to pass up water from the stage to the
President's box—others try to clamber up—&c., &c., &c.

"In the midst of all this the soldiers of the President's
Guard, with others, suddenly drawn to the scene, burst
in—some 200 altogether—they storm the house, through
all the tiers, especially the upper ones, inflamed with fury,
literally charging the audience with fixed bayonets, muskets and pistols, shouting "Clear out! clear out!—you
sons of b—!" Such the wild scene, or a suggestion of it
rather, inside the play house that night.

"Outside, too, in the atmosphere of shock and craze, crowds of people, filled with frenzy, ready to seize any outlet for it, came near committing murder several times on innocent individuals. One such case was especially exciting. The infuriated crowd, through some chance, got started against one man, either for words he uttered, or perhaps without any cause at all, and were proceeding at once to actually hang him on a neighboring lamp post, when he was rescued by a few heroic policemen, who placed him in their midst and fought their way slowly and amid great peril toward the station house. It was a fitting episode of the whole affair. The crowd rushing and eddying to and fro—the night, the yells, the pale faces, many frightened people trying in vain to extricate themselves—the attacked man, not yet freed from the jaws of death, looking like a corpse—the silent, resolute half dozen policemen, with no weapons but their little clubs, yet stern and steady through all those eddying swarms— made indeed a fitting side scene to the grand tragedy of the murder. They gained the station house with the protected man, whom they placed in security for the night, and discharged him in the morning.

"And in the midst of that night pandemonium of senseless hate, infuriated soldiers, the audience, and the crowd—the stage, and all its actors and actresses, its paint pots, spangles, and gas lights—the life blood from those veins, the best and sweetest of the land, drips slowly down, and death's ooze already begins its little bubbles on the lips.

"Such, hurriedly sketched, were the accompaniments of the death of President Lincoln. So suddenly, and in murder and horror unsurpassed, he was taken from us. But his death was painless."

[9]The original of this letter is owned by Oscar Lion of New York, to whom I am indebted for this copy.

[10]Perry, p. 224; Binns, p. 270; Platt, p. 84; Bucke, p. 22.

[11]*Complete Works*, p. 506.

[12]This document gives the address as first orally delivered. While it repeats verbatim the essential parts of the article in the *New York Sun* of February 12, 1876, it marks the transition of Walt's idea from that of a chapter in a book to a spoken discourse. It has other interesting variations which the careful student will note with interest. This is the address which Mr. Slade and I at first thought was an undiscovered lecture by Whitman, and the one which started me on the quest whose outcome is this book. It appeared in the *New York Tribune* of April 15, 1879.

More than three years had gone by since Walt published the substance of this in the expectation of making a book about Lincoln. He did not find his strength and resolution equal to that undertaking; but he did find himself in such condition of health he thought possibly he might still have a career as a lecturer. He had not much material out of which he could hope to make new books, and the representatives of the Society for the Suppression of Vice were indisposed to help him sell new editions of *Leaves of Grass*, but people were curious to see him, and liked to hear him tell about Lincoln. This is what he told them in New York in 1879, and, with such modifications as are shown in the final draft, this is what he continued to deliver almost once a year as long as he lived:

"THE DEATH OF LINCOLN
"A LECTURE BY
"WALT WHITMAN

"Though by no means proposing to resume the Secession War to-night, I would briefly remind you, my friends, of the public conditions preceding that contest. For twenty years, and especially during the four or five before the war actually began, the aspect of affairs in the United States, though without the flash of military excitement, presents more than the survey of a battle, or any campaign, or series even of Nature's convulsions. The hot passions of the South—the strange mixture at the North of inertia, incredulity, and conscious power—the incendiarism of the Abolitionists—the rascality and grip of the politicians, unparalleled in any land, any age. To these, I must not omit adding the honesty of the essential bulk of the people everywhere—yet with all the seething fury and contradiction of their natures more aroused than the Atlantic's waves in wildest equinox.

"What could be more ominous (though generally unappreciated then) what more significant than the Presidentials of Filmore and Buchanan? Proving conclusively that the weakness and wickedness of elected rulers, backed by our great parties, are just as likely to afflict us here, as in the countries of the Old World, under their monarchies, emperors and aristocracies. In that Old World were everywhere heard underground rumblings, that died out, only again sure to return. While in America the volcano though civic yet, continued to grow more and more convulsive—more and more stormy and threatening.

"In the height of all this excitement and chaos, hovering on the edge at first, and then merged in its very midst, and destined to play a leading part, appears a strange and awkward figure.

"I shall not easily forget the first time I ever saw Abraham Lincoln. It must have been about the eighteenth or nineteenth of February, 1861. It was rather a pleasant afternoon in New York City, as he arrived here from the West, to remain a few hours, and then pass on

to Washington, to prepare for his inauguration. I saw
him in Broadway, near the site of the present Post-Office.
He came down, I think, from Canal Street, to stop at the
Astor House. The broad spaces, sidewalks and street
in the neighborhood for some distance, were crowded with
solid masses of people—many thousands. The omnibuses and other vehicles had all been turned off, leaving
an unusual hush in that busy part of the city. Presently
two or three shabby hack barouches made their way with
some difficulty through the crowd and drew up at the
Astor House entrance. A tall figure stepped out of the
center of these barouches, paused leisurely on the sidewalk, looked up at the dark granite walls, and looming
architecture of the grand old hotel—then, after a relieving stretch of arms and legs, turned round for over a
minute to scan slowly and good-humoredly the appearance of the vast and silent crowds. There were no
speeches—no compliments—no welcome—as far as I could
hear, not a word said. Still much anxiety was concealed
in that quiet. Cautious persons had feared some marked
insult or indignity to the President-elect—for he
possessed no personal popularity at all in New York City,
and very little political. But it was evidently tacitly
agreed that if the few political supporters of Mr. Lincoln
present would abstain from any demonstration on their
side, the immense majority who were anything but supporters, would abstain on their side also. The result was
a sulky unbroken silence, such as certainly never before
characterized so great a New York crowd.

"Almost in the same neighborhood I distinctly remembered seeing Lafayette on his visit to America in 1825. I
had also personally seen and heard how Andrew Jackson,
Clay, Webster, Hungarian Kossuth, Filibuster Walker,
the Prince of Wales on his visit, and other celebres, native
and foreign, had been welcomed there at various times—

all that indescribable roar and magnetism, unlike any
other sound in the universe, the glad exulting thunder-
shouts of countless unloosed throats of men: but on this
occasion, not a voice—not a sound:

"From the top of an omnibus, (driven up one side,
close by, and blocked by the curbstone and the crowds)
I had, I say, a capital view of it all, and especially of
Mr. Lincoln, his look and gait—his perfect composure
and coolness—his unusual and uncouth height, his dress
of complete black, stovepipe hat pushed back on his
head, his dark brown complexion, seamed and wrinkled,
yet canny-looking face, his black, bushy head of hair,
disproportionately long neck, and his hands held behind
as he stood observing the people. He looked with
curiosity upon that immense sea of faces, and the sea
of faces returned the look with similar curiosity. In both
there was a dash of comedy, almost farce, such as
Shakespeare put in his blackest tragedies. The crowd
that hemmed round, consisted, I should think, of thirty
to forty thousand men, not a single one his personal
friend—while I have no doubt (so frenzied were the
ferments of the time) many an assassin's knife and pistol
lurked in hip or breast pocket there, ready soon as break
and riot came.

"But no break or riot came. The tall figure gave
another relieving stretch or two of arms and legs: then
with moderate pace, and accompanied by a few unknown-
looking persons, ascended the portico steps of the Astor
House, disappeared through its broad entrance—and the
dumb show ended.

"I saw Abraham Lincoln often the four years following that date. He changed rapidly and much during his
Presidency—but this scene and him in it, are indelibly
stamped upon my recollection. As I sat on the top of my
omnibus, and had a good view of him, the thought, dim

and inchoate then, has since been clear enough, that four sorts of genius—four mighty and primal hands, will be needed to the complete limning of this man's future portrait—the eyes and brains and fingertouch of Plutarch and Æschylus and Michael Angelo, assisted by Rabelais.

"THE WAR AND THE MURDER

"And now, (Mr. Lincoln passing on from this scene to Washington, where he was inaugurated, amid armed cavalry, and sharpshooters at every point—the first instance of the kind in our history, and I hope it will be the last), now the rapid succession of well-known events, too well known, I believe, these days, we almost hate to hear them mentioned—the National flag fired on at Sumter, the uprising of the North in paroxysms of astonishment and rage, the chaos of divided counsels, the call for troops, the first Bull Run, the stunning castdown, shock and dismay of the North; and so in full the Secession War. Four years of lurid, bleeding, murky, murderous war. Why paint those years, with all their scenes?—the hard-fought engagements—the defeats, plans, failures—the gloomy hours, days when our Nationality seemed hung in a pall of doubt, perhaps death—the Mephistophelian sneers of foreign lands and attachés—the dreaded Scylla of European interference, and the Charybdis of the tremendously dangerous latent strata of secession sympathizers throughout the Free States (far more numerous than is supposed)—the long marches in summer—the hot sweat, and many a sunstroke, as on the rush to Gettysbury in 1863, the night battles in the woods, as under Hooker at Chancellorsville (a strange episode!)—the camps in winter—the military prisons—the hospitals,—alas! alas! the hospitals!)

"The Secession War? Nay, let me call it the Union War. Though whatever called, it is even yet too near us—too vast and too closely overshadowing—its branches unformed, yet (but certain) shooting too far into the future—and the most indicative and mightiest of them yet ungrown.

"A great literature will yet arise out of the era of those four years, those scenes—era compressing centuries of native passion, first-class pictures, tempests of life and death, an inexhaustible mine for the histories, drama, romance and even philosophy of peoples to come, indeed the verteber of poetry and art (of personal character too) for all future America—far more grand, in my opinion, to the hands capable of it, than Homer's Siege of Troy, or the French Wars to Shakespeare.

"But I must leave these speculations and come to the theme I have assigned and limited myself to.

"Of the actual murder of President Lincoln, though so much has been written, probably the facts are yet very indefinite in most persons' minds. I read from my memoranda, already published, written at the time on the spot, and revised frequently and finally since.

"The day, April 14, 1865, seems to have been a pleasant one throughout the whole land—the moral atmosphere pleasant too—the long storm so dark, so fratricidal, full of blood and doubt and gloom, over and ended at last, by the sunrise of such an absolute National victory, and utter breakdown of secession—we almost doubted our own senses! Early herbage, early flowers were out. (I remember where I was stopping at the time; the season being advanced, there were many lilacs in full bloom. By one of those caprices that enter and give tinge to events without being at all a part of them, I find myself always reminded of the great tragedy of that day by the sight and odor of these blossoms. It never fails.)

"But I must not dwell on accessories. The deed hastens. The popular afternoon paper of Washington, the little *Evening Star*, had spattered all over its third page, divided among the advertisements in a sensational manner in a hundred places, 'The President and his Lady will be at the Theatre this evening.' (Lincoln was fond of the theatre. I have myself seen him there several times. I remember thinking how funny it was that he, in some respects, the leading actor in the stormiest drama known to real history's stage, through centuries, should sit there and be so completely interested and absorbed in those jack-straws, moving about with their silly little gestures, foreign spirit, and flatulent text.)

"On this occasion the theatre was crowded, many ladies in rich and gay costumes, officers in their uniforms, many well-known citizens, young folks, the usual clusters of gas lights, the usual magnetism of so many people, cheerful, with perfumes, music of violins and flutes—(and over all, and saturating all, that vast vague wonder, *VICTORY*, the Nation's Victory, the triumph of the Union, filling the air, the thought, the sense, with exhilaration more than all music and perfumes.

"The President came betimes, and, with his wife, witnessed the play from the large stage-boxes of the second tier, two thrown into one, and profusely draped with the National flag. There is a scene in the play representing a modern parlor, in which two unprecedented English ladies are informed by an impossible Yankee that he is not a man of fortune, and therefore undesirable for marriage-catching purposes; after which, the comments being finished, the dramatic trio make exit, leaving the stage clear for the moment. At this period came the murder of Abraham Lincoln. Great as that was, with

all its manifold train, circling round it, and stretching
into the future for many a century, in the politics,
history, art, etc., of the New World, in point of fact, the
main thing, the actual murder, transpired with the quiet
and simplicity of any commonest occurrence—the bursting of a bud or pod in the growth of vegetation, for
instance. Through the general hum following the stage
pause, with the change of positions came the sound of a
muffled pistol shot, which not one hundredth part of the
audience heard at the time,—and yet a moment's hush—
somehow, surely a vague startled thrill—and then,
through the ornamented, draperied, starred and striped
spaceway of the President's box, a sudden figure, a man
raises himself with hands and feet, stands a moment on the
railing, leaps below to the stage, (a distance of perhaps
fourteen or fifteen feet), falls out of his position, catching his boot-heel in a copious drapery, (the American
flag), falls on one knee, quickly recovers himself, rises as
if nothing had happened, (he really sprains his ankle, but
unfelt then)—and so the figure, Booth, the murderer,
dressed in plain black broadcloth, bareheaded, with a full
head of glossy raven hair, and his eyes like some mad
animal's, flashing with light and resolution, yet with a
certain calmness, holds aloft in one hand a large knife—
walks along not much back from the footlights—turns
fully toward the audience his face of statuesque beauty,
lit by those basilisk eyes, flashing with desperation, perhaps insanity—launches out in a firm and steady voice
the words, *Sic semper tyrannis*—and then walks with
neither slow nor very rapid pace diagonally across the
back of the stage and disappears. (Had not all this
terrible scene—making the mimic ones preposterous—had
it not all been rehearsed, in blank, by Booth beforehand?)

"A moment's hush—a scream—the cry of *Murder*—
Mrs. Lincoln leaning out of the box, with ashy cheeks **and**

lips, with involuntary cry, pointing to the retreating figure, *He has kill'd the President* . . . and still a moment's strange, incredulous suspense—and then the deluge!—then that mixture of horror, noises, uncertainty—(the sound, somewhere back, of a horse's hoofs clattering with speed)—the people burst through chairs and railings, and break them up—that noise adds to the queerness of these scenes—there is inextricable confusion and terror, women faint—quite feeble persons fall and are trampled on—many cries of agony are heard—the broad stage suddenly fills to suffocation with a dense and motley crowd, like some horrible carnival—the audience rush generally upon it—at least the strong men do—the actors and actresses are there in their play costumes and painted faces, with mortal fright showing through the rouge, some trembling, some in tears, the screams, and calls, and confused talk—redoubled, trebled—two or three manage to pass up water from the stage to the President's box—others try to clamber up, etc, etc.

"In the midst of all this, the soldiers of the President's Guard, with others suddenly drawn to the scene, burst in—(some two hundred altogether)—they storm the house, through all the tiers, especially the upper ones, inflamed with fury, literally charging the audience with fixed bayonets, muskets and pistols, shouting *Clear out! clear out! you sons of* ——. . . . Such the wild scene, or a suggestion of it rather, inside the play-house.

"And in that night-pandemonium of senseless hate, infuriated soldiers, the audience and the crowd—the stage and all its actors and actresses, its paint-pots, spangles, and gas-lights,—the life-blood from those veins, the best and sweetest of the land, drips slowly down, and death's ooze already begins its little bubbles on the lips.

"Results of the Tragedy

"Thus the visible incidents and surroundings of President Lincoln's murder, as they really occurred. Thus ended the attempted secessions of these States. Thus the four years' war. But the main things come subtly and invisibly afterward—perhaps long afterward—neither military, political, not (great as those are) historical. I say, certain secondary and indirect results, out of the war, and out of the tragedy of his death, are, in my opinion, greatest. Not the event of the murder itself. Not that Mr. Lincoln strings the principal points and personages of the period, like beads, upon the single string of his career. Not that his idiosyncrasy, in its sudden appearance and disappearance, stamps the Republic with a stamp more marked and enduring than any yet given by any one man—(more even than Washington's). But, joined with these, the immeasurable value and meaning of that whole tragedy lies, to me, in senses finally dearest to a Nation (and here all our own)—the imaginative and the artistic senses—the literary and the dramatic ones. Not in any common or low meaning of those terms, but a meaning precious to the race and to every age. A long and varied series of contradictory events arrives at last at its highest poetic, single, central, pictorial denouement. The whole, involved, baffling, multiform whirl of the secession period comes to a head, and is gathered in one brief flash of lightning-illumination—one simple, fierce deed. Its sharp culmination and, as it were, solution of so many bloody and angry problems, illustrates those climax moments on the stage of universal Time, where the Historic Muse at one entrance, and the Tragic Muse at the other, suddenly ringing down the curtain, close an immense act in the long drama of creative thought, and give it radiation, tableau, stranger than fiction. Fit radiation—fit close! How the imagination—how the student loves these things! America, too, is to have them. For not in all great deaths, nor far or near—not Cæsar in the Roman Senate house, nor Napoleon passing away in the wild night-storm at St. Helena—not Palaeologus, falling, desperately fighting, piled over dozens deep with Grecian corpses—not calm old Socrates, drinking the hemlock—outvies that terminus of the Secession War, in one man's life, here in our midst, in our own time—that seal of the emancipation of three million slaves—that parturition and delivery of our new-born, at least really free Republic, henceforth to commence its career of genuine homogeneous Union, compact, consistent with itself.

"Nor will ever future American patriots and Unionists, indifferently over the whole land, or North or South, find a better seal to their lesson. The final use of the greatest men of a nation is, after all, not with reference to their deeds in themselves, or their direct bearing on their times or lands. The final use of a heroic-eminent life—especially of a heroic-eminent death—is its indirect filtering into the nation and the race, and to give, often at many removes, but unerringly, age after age, color and fiber to the personalism of the youth and maturity of that age, and of mankind. Then there is a cement to the whole people, subtler, more underlying than anything in written Constitution, or courts or armies—namely, the cement of a death identified thoroughly with that people at its head, and for its sake. Strange (is it not?) that battles, martyrs, agonies, blood, even assassinations, should so condense—perhaps only really, lastingly condense—a nationality.

"I repeat it—the grand deaths of the race—the dramatic deaths of every nationality—are its most important inheritance—(by them) value, in some respects, beyond its literature and art—(as the hero is beyond his finest portrait, and the battle itself beyond its choicest song or epic). Is not here indeed the point underlying all tragedy? the famous pieces of the Grecian Masters—and all masters? Why if the old Greeks had had this man, what trilogies of plays—what epics—would have been made out of him! How the rhapsodies would have recited him! How quickly that quaint tall form would have entered into the region where men vitalize gods, and gods divinify men!

"When, centuries hence (as it must, in my opinion, be centuries hence before the life of these States, or of democracy, can be really written and illustrated) the leading historians and dramatists seek for some personage, some special event, incisive enough to mark with the deepest cut, and mnemonize this turbulent nineteenth century of ours (not only these States, but all over the political and social world)—something, perhaps, to close that gorgeous procession of European feudalism, with all its pomp and caste prejudices, of whose long train we in America are yet so inextricably the heirs—something to identify with terrible identification, by far the greatest revolutionary step in the United States (perhaps the greatest of the world, our century) the absolute extirpation and erasure of slavery from the States—those historians will seek in vain for any point to serve more thoroughly their purpose than Abraham Lincoln's death.

"Dear to the Muse—thrice dear to Nationality, to the whole human race, precious to this Union, precious to democracy—unspeakably and forever precious—their first great martyr chief."

[13]Bucke refers to this lecture, p. 68. Perry gives a facsimile of one of the initialed tickets, facing page 224.

[14]*Complete Prose Works*, pp. 301-307.

[15]Perry, p. 227; Bucke, p. 224; Kennedy, p. 3.

[16]Binns, p. 317; Donaldson, p. 103; Kennedy, p. 6.

[17]William Sloan Kennedy, *Reminiscences of Walt Whitman*, p. 25.

[18]*With Walt Whitman at Camden*, Vol. II, p. 438.

[19]Perry, p. 252; Binns, p. 317.

[20]*Walt Whitman, Poet and Friend*, pp. 156-157.

[21]*Life of John Hay*, by William Roscoe Thayer, Volume II., p. 42.

[22]*Reminiscences of Walt Whitman*, p. 35.

[23]Binns, p. 332; Perry, p. 255.

[24]When Whitman delivered this lecture for the last time, in Philadelphia, on Tuesday night, April 15, 1890, he wrote a new introduction, which was given to the *Boston Transcript*, and appeared in that paper. This opening section, written for the twenty-fifth anniversary of the assassination, reads:

"THE FINAL INTRODUCTION

"Of Abraham Lincoln, bearing testimony twenty-five years after his death—and of that death—I am now, my friends, before you. Few realize the days, the great historic and esthetic personalities, with him as their center, we passed through. Abraham Lincoln, familiar, our own, an Illinoisan, modern, yet tallying ancient Moses, Joshua, or later Cromwell, and grander in some respects than any of them; Abraham Lincoln, that makes the life of Homer, Plutarch, Shakspeare, eligible our day or any day. My subject this evening for forty or fifty minutes talk is the death of this man, and how that death will finally filter into America. I am not going to tell you anything new: and it is doubtless nearly altogether because I ardently wish to commemorate the hour and martyrdom I now am here. Oft as the rolling years bring back this hour, let it again, however briefly, be dwelt upon. For my part, I intend, until my own dying day, whenever the fourteenth or fifteenth of April comes, to annually gather a few friends and hold its tragic reminiscence. No narrow or sectional reminiscence. It belongs to these States in their entirety—not the North only, but the South—perhaps belongs most tenderly and devotedly to the South, of all; for there really this man's birthstock; there and then his antecedents stamp. Why should I say that thence his manliest traits, his universality, his canny, easy words upon the surface,—his inflexible determination at heart? Have you ever realized it, my friends, that Lincoln, though grafted on the West, is essentially in personel and character a Southern contribution?"

INDEX

INDEX

271